YOU CAN CALL ME STAN

This book is dedicated to my wife Paulina

YOU CAN CALL ME STAN

THE STILIYAN PETROV STORY

Stiliyan Petrov with Mark Guidi
Foreword by Martin O'Neill

MAINSTREAM
PUBLISHING
EDINBURGH AND LONDON

First published in Great Britain in 2005 by
MAINSTREAM PUBLISHING COMPANY (EDINBURGH) LTD
7 Albany Street
Edinburgh EH1 3UG

ISBN 1 84596 074 2

A catalogue record for this book
is available from the British Library

Typeset in Apollo

Printed and bound in Great Britain by
Clays Ltd, St Ives plc

Acknowledgements

Thanks to Celtic Football Club and Mainstream Publishing. At Celtic, Peter Lawwell, Iain Jamieson and Rhona MacDonald have been helpful and considerate at all times. A big thanks to them. At Mainstream, the contribution of Bill Campbell, Graeme Blaikie, Paul Murphy and Sharon Atherton has been huge.

To Stiliyan, my son. You've no idea how happy you make me feel.

To Mum, Dad and Ivan. Thanks for being beside me when it mattered.

Thanks to my Celtic teammates, past and present, for helping me every day.

Special thanks to Martin O'Neill for providing a considered foreword.

Thanks to the *Sunday Mail*, particularly the Sports Desk and Picture Desk. The input of Frank Murphy, Austin Barrett and David McKie is much appreciated.

A huge thank you to Brian McSweeney. Brian, your contribution was vital.

The most important man of all has been Brian Wilson. A true friend. It wouldn't have been possible without you.

Mark Guidi is the *Sunday Mail*'s Chief Football Writer. He has been with the paper since 1995. He is also a pundit on Radio Clyde's popular *Super Scoreboard* programme.

Mark lives with his wife Anne and their two daughters, Eva and Sophia.

Contents

Foreword by Martin O'Neill OBE   9

1. Signing for Celtic   13
2. The Day I Quit Celtic   25
3. My Favourite Team – Me, Paulina and Stiliyan, jun.   37
4. Growing Up in Bulgaria   45
5. The Army   57
6. My Celtic Managers   67
7. My Leg Break and Weird Superstitions   81
8. The Old Firm   95
9. Seville   127
10. European Adventures   145
11. Euro 2004   173
12. The National Team   181
13. My Favourite Games   189
14. My Fantasy XI   201
15. 72 Hours in My Life   209
16. You Can Call Me Stan but Not a Diver   219
17. Charity Work and Future Plans   227

Foreword

It was the first week of July 2000, I was one month into my reign as the manager of Celtic and the players were returning for the dreaded pre-season training. I was to meet for the first time a fresh-faced, tanned, handsome young man. I didn't know it then but this particular lad was to have a major influence on the direction of the football club for the next five years of its wonderful history.

However, what I did know immediately was that with such good looks he'd be an instant hit in our household. My two daughters Aisling and Alana, having spent much of their young lives in the midst of professional footballers, were forever encouraging me to sign handsome young men or blinking well go to a club that already possessed them.

In the summer of 1999, Stiliyan Petrov left his home and family behind in Bulgaria to begin a professional football career in Scotland. Unable to speak much English but armed with a pair of football boots and a great desire to make the grade, he arrived in Glasgow. Early life in the city was, naturally, pretty lonely. Missing his family and unable to grasp the Scottish culture, he took some time to settle. But he was certainly coming to terms with the life by the time I had been introduced to him that early July morning.

I felt that if he was prepared to sacrifice life at home in Bulgaria at such a tender age in order to prove himself in another country, he would surely possess the mental toughness and determination necessary to overcome the many hurdles that professional football would put in his way. Over the next five seasons, he would prove that point, time and time again.

Strangely enough, for someone who is now considered to be an extremely fit player – with the ability to get more easily than most from box to box – Stiliyan's fitness gave me cause for concern in those early days. In fact, on the second day of training, he was one of the first players to drop out of a running exercise designed to monitor early performance levels.

I think I may well have voiced such concerns to him that very day, but Stiliyan just smiled at me, as only Stiliyan can, and told me not to worry. He said, 'I will be ready when it's necessary.' That was enough for me.

His commanding presence on the training ground and on the big stage itself is the quality that he possesses that sets him apart. No Celtic side in the past five years has been at full strength without the inclusion of Stiliyan. His teammates always want to see Stiliyan's name on the team-sheet. He has been a major influence on the team, and his apparent shyness has disappeared. He has a voice in the dressing-room worth listening to, and he commands total respect from his peers.

Stiliyan's importance to Celtic has grown over the seasons and that, in the main, is down to the man himself. Big attempts by him to improve the use of his left foot were followed by even bigger efforts to improve the defensive side of his game, but he is really an attack-minded player with the ability to score goals. This goal-scoring ability is, in itself, an enormous asset, especially as he mostly scores important goals, not the last in a 5–0 victory.

I'll never forget the one he scored against Rangers in a wonderful 6–2 victory in my first Old Firm game as manager of the football club – Stiliyan got our second goal. I'm still convinced to this day that victory gave us the belief to go on and win the championship and eventually the Treble, thereby ending Rangers' domination of the Scottish game. When he opened his scoring account, during my time as manager of Celtic, we all felt that many more would quickly follow. Scoring spectacular goals, and there have been many, has been his speciality. However, his main concern is ensuring that Celtic and Bulgaria – whom he now captains – win.

My honest belief is that he possesses the ability to become one of Europe's best midfield players – he is that exceptional. Anyway, I wish him well. I will miss him greatly – his character, his dedication and his smile. However, I will not always miss his moaning. My word, he enjoyed a tantrum or complaint if the mood took him. Perhaps that is also part of the make-up that makes him the great player that he undoubtedly is. Come to think of it then, I'll miss his moaning as well.

Martin O'Neill OBE

1

Signing for Celtic

I first discovered that Celtic were interested in signing me during my summer holiday in Sunny Beach at the Bulgarian seaside in the summer of 1999. I was lying on the sand enjoying the sunshine, but I didn't know where my future lay, and I couldn't even find out because I'd switched off my mobile phone, unable to afford the bill! It was a roasting hot day and I was sleeping off a hangover after a night of drinking with some of my teammates from CSKA Sofia, whom I was playing for at the time. It was the close season, and we were celebrating the fact that we had just won the Bulgarian Cup. The season before that, we had won the League Championship and the Bulgarian Cup to do the Double.

The news that someone wanted to sign me came just after I had played for the national side in the 1–1 draw against England in a European Championship qualifier for the Euro 2000 finals, in Sofia on 9 June. By all accounts, Celtic had been tipped off about me a couple of months earlier, and the new management regime of John Barnes and Kenny Dalglish had sent their scouts to watch me play against England. Following a favourable report, and after watching some video footage of me in action, Celtic decided they wanted to bring me to Glasgow. Werder Bremen, Roma and Panathinaikos had also informed my agent they were interested in signing me.

Thankfully, Ilia Pavlov, the president of CSKA Sofia who is sadly no longer with us, used his amazing network of contacts to track me down. After less than 24 hours, one of his members of staff had found me on the beach after contacting one of my friends on his mobile. If the president hadn't had such an extensive network of contacts in Bulgaria then I probably wouldn't have made it to Celtic – it would have been about three weeks before I would have had enough money to get my mobile working again!

I was told to leave the seaside and get back to the club immediately. However, I wasn't told that Celtic had bid for me; I was just informed that a famous European club had offered a transfer fee to buy me from CSKA. So I went back to the city, and the president told me that Celtic wanted me to join them. My first reaction was that I didn't believe it was going to happen. I had been linked with many clubs in the Bulgarian papers, and there were stories appearing every day about me leaving for here, there and everywhere. I was a bit fed up with it to be honest and had almost had enough. Werder Bremen's interest was really strong at that time – as it had been for a couple of months – and I did start to think about what it would be like to play in the *Bundesliga*.

As soon as I had arrived back in Sofia to meet the CSKA President I knew there was something going down, and it soon transpired that the negotiations to sell me to Celtic were nearing completion. I was really surprised about their interest as I didn't think a top team from Scotland would be interested in a 19-year-old Bulgarian. At that moment, I had hundreds of thoughts rushing through my head, and if I had to make a decision there and then, I would have opted *not* to go. I knew a little bit about Celtic but didn't know anything about Scotland and what it would be like to live there. I was nervous and a little bit scared. It was as if everything had been agreed and I *had* to go to Celtic. It all seemed so rushed, but I wasn't going to be forced to go anywhere. I needed to take a step back and think a lot about this move.

Naturally, I had ambitions to go and play abroad, and when I was a kid I used to see the success Hristo Stoichkov was having in Spain with Barcelona. I had dreams of going there and being as renowned as he was when Barca lifted the 1992 European Cup and he won the European Footballer of the Year award in 1995. From an early age, Hristo was my inspiration. His success as a footballer gave me the hunger and desire to go on and have a career in football. I wanted to work hard, train like a top professional and play well to have a career as successful as he had.

However, at that time, I felt I was going to be with CSKA for at least two more years. I was happy to stay with the club and let myself develop a bit more as a person and a footballer. It's a bit different now: young footballers in Bulgaria can't get out of the country quick enough to play in a more high-profile league. They are much more ambitious and, dare I say it, a little bit more cheeky than I was when I was a teenager.

I had watched Old Firm games on the television and knew a bit about Scottish football, but it was only a little bit and not enough to make me want to give up what I had in Bulgaria and set up home in Scotland. I remembered watching one Old Firm game in particular and being very impressed with Simon Donnelly, but I was told he was no longer at the club, having moved to Sheffield Wednesday on a Bosman transfer.

I didn't really want to move away to another country where I would have no friends and wouldn't be able to speak the language. I thought there was no way I would be happy. I talked the move over with my parents and explained it was going to be a massive step to move away. My father told me that if I wanted to be a top footballer and earn a good living from the game, I had to take this chance. Deep down, it was probably what I wanted to hear, and the fact that the advice came from my father made it feel like the right thing to do. If you can't take advice from your father you have a problem. That night I went to bed and slept on it. Well, when I say slept, that's not really correct because I tossed and turned all night, thinking about the huge decision I needed to make.

CSKA got in touch the next day to tell me that they had agreed terms with Celtic and that I was expected in Glasgow for a medical. It was decision time. I took a deep breath and said, 'OK, I'm going to go for it.'

I had to quickly pack my bag, and it was only then it struck me what few clothes I possessed. I had a little holdall and packed a couple of T-shirts, trousers, a jumper, some underwear, a jacket and a pair of shoes. Apart from the clothes on my back, and about £10 in my wallet, that was really all I took with me. I got on the plane with Milen Petkov, my teammate from CSKA and the national side, as he had the chance of signing for Celtic, too. It was great to have him there, because he was a friend as well as a teammate.

We arrived in Glasgow on 14 June 1999. All the Celtic fans seemed to recognise me and Petkov straight away, and whenever we walked through the streets, people would shout at us to sign for the club and help Celtic win prizes. It was amazing but also hard to comprehend that so many people had taken to me without even seeing me kick a ball in a Celtic jersey.

Our visit turned a bit sour when Petkov decided to turn down Celtic's offer. He wasn't happy with some details in the contract, and I understood his reasons as he was 25 and had a family to support. He was right not to move them to a new country under conditions he wasn't 100 per cent happy with. It was slightly different for me as I was single, and this was my big chance to play in another European country. That was all that interested me, although my priorities changed shortly after I signed for Celtic when I realised that my finances were tight. Very tight. At first, though, it was fantastic.

Before I signed, I decided to use the most famous phone number in my little red address book and got in touch with Hristo Stoichkov. I had already played with him at international level and with the experience he had in the game, it would have been crazy not to talk my move over with him. As it turned out, he encouraged me to move to Glasgow and told me that when he left Bulgaria for the first time to play abroad he was nervous but knew he had to do it. Joining Barcelona made him a better player and a better person and he has never for a moment regretted his decision. Of course, Hristo still lives in Barcelona and is now the national team manager of Bulgaria.

He told me that I wouldn't regret leaving Bulgaria and that I should ignore the offers from other clubs as playing for Celtic would help me to develop into one of Bulgaria's best-ever midfielders. I was pleased and flattered to hear him say that. After all, this is a guy who is rated as the best footballer my country has ever produced, and there he was praising me! Before he took over the Bulgaria job he was in constant contact, and I'm proud to call him a friend and someone I can to talk to in confidence.

I also spoke to Ilian Kiriakov, who played for Aberdeen, and asked him his advice and thoughts on Scotland and Scottish football. He told me Celtic were a huge club and that I had to sign for them as I would regret it for the rest of my life if I didn't.

The negotiations were dragging on a little in Glasgow between my then agent Tanev Latchezar and the Celtic powerbrokers. I began to get nervous about this and thought the deal was about to collapse. The more it dragged on the more pressure I felt on me. The Bulgarian press and television were on the phone every day pestering me, trying to find out when the deal would be 100 per cent official. The club tried to keep me occupied by taking me on a tour of Celtic Park and the club museum and showing me the different sights around Glasgow, such as Hampden Park and the fancy shopping centres. I was a bit gobsmacked by it all as there was nothing like it in Bulgaria.

Eventually, it all came together and my agent managed to negotiate a deal he felt wasn't too bad. Before I signed, my agent looked me in the eye and asked me, 'Do you want to sign this? Do you really want to move here?' I answered 'Yes' and put pen to paper in a room at the Glasgow Thistle Hotel on 18 June. I was delighted I'd finalised my big move but sad that Petkov didn't sign.

You Can Call Me Stan

We had spent nearly a week together, and throughout that time, our friendship had grown stronger. It would have been fantastic to play for Celtic together and continue our friendship.

The build-up to the moment when I actually put pen to paper had been nerve-racking, and there were times I wasn't sure it was ever going to happen. The day I came over from Bulgaria I was told I'd be signing the next day and then it was put off to the next day. And then the day after that. And the day after that. I eventually signed five days after arriving in Glasgow.

We stayed at Cameron House for the first couple of days and that was beautiful. The scenery there is fantastic, and, these days, I try to go down there for a day trip whenever I have time. After Cameron House, Celtic moved us to the Thistle Hotel in Glasgow city centre. I even remember my room number – room 310. I met the then Celtic boss John Barnes on the second night and we had dinner together.

He had a glass of wine with his meal and told me that it was OK for me to have a glass also, but I declined his offer. I was nervous about drinking alcohol in front of him. I didn't know whether he might have been testing me to see if I liked a drink. So I thought it was safer and more professional not to take anything, and I just had a Coca-Cola.

We talked through an interpreter about Celtic and what Barnes wanted me to do for the team, discussing what position he wanted me to play. He had watched my performance for Bulgaria in our match against England and had earmarked me for a role in central midfield.

I was impressed with Barnes. I knew of him from his playing days with Liverpool and England. He is a legend in English football, and I was well aware that this was his first job in management. During that initial meeting, I honestly felt that he would go on and crack the dominance that Rangers had enjoyed for the best part of a decade by helping Celtic to win the league. But, of course, it didn't turn out that way, and my opinion of him deteriorated rapidly as the months passed.

However, when I first met him, he painted a very good picture of Celtic and told me he planned to make Rangers work really hard for success that year. He told me Celtic had good players and that I would settle into life in Glasgow easily and would quickly learn to speak English. That gave me a good lift, and from that moment on, I was desperate to get on with my new job.

After I signed the five-year contract, I had to return to Bulgaria until my visa application was sorted out. That too dragged on, and I was a worried man back home. My football future lay in the hands of some civil servants and that made me feel anxious and unsettled. To take my mind off it, I partied with my friends at Sunny Beach for ten days to celebrate my new job and what I hoped would be the start of a great new chapter in my career.

However, the party atmosphere quickly fizzled out when I discovered that my first visa application had been rejected. It took nearly seven weeks until it was eventually sorted out. Those seven weeks not playing football or training properly seemed like an eternity, although I did fly to Germany with CSKA to do pre-season training and that helped me. Thankfully, Kevin Keegan, who was England manager at that time, submitted an excellent reference on my behalf to the Department of Employment. Thanks to that and some other paperwork submitted by Celtic and the Bulgarian FA, I managed to get the legalities sorted out, and I was on my way to Glasgow.

My mother was very worried about me moving, and I remember the night before I was due to leave for Glasgow she came into my room and gave me a big cuddle. She cried and told me she was worried about me going to live in a strange place with people I didn't know. I was also worried but didn't want her to know. She had to accept that I was a professional footballer and that I couldn't stay in Bulgaria forever. I told her everything was going to be fine and that my move to Scotland was going to be the best thing that ever happened to me. To be honest, I wasn't sure if that was going to be the case and I confessed to my father that the fact Celtic were paying around £2.8 million worried me. The fee made me the most expensive player in the history of Bulgarian football, breaking the previous record of £2 million that CSKA had received from Barcelona for Stoichkov nine years earlier. I was only 19 and another club was paying this huge amount of money for me. My father told me to forget about the fee and just concentrate on playing football. My brother Ivan was also worried about me, but he was more interested to know how much money I was going to earn so he'd have an idea how much extra pocket money I'd be sending him back!

About a year before my move to Celtic, my very good friend Martin Petrov left Bulgaria to sign for Servette in Switzerland. I went with him to the airport just before his move. When we were saying our final goodbyes he burst into tears, and I told him he should stop behaving like a woman and finish with the crying, but he couldn't. I should have kept my mouth shut, because when I was on my way out of the airport that afternoon, I started to cry. I was worrying about him and how difficult life was going to be and how he was going to cope on his own in a strange country. I vowed there and then that if I ever got the chance to leave Bulgaria and was waving goodbye to my friends and family, I wouldn't cry. Martin is now doing very well in Spain with Atlético Madrid.

Of course, when the day came for me to leave for good and move to Glasgow, I couldn't stop myself from crying. It was Thursday, 5 August and my mother, father and brother were all at the airport to see me off. They were all sobbing, which started me off – we couldn't help it. It was such an emotional time and one I'll never forget.

When I was on the plane, I had second thoughts, and if the pilot had offered me the chance to pull on a parachute and jump off, I reckon I would have. But there was no way back. I knew I had to be strong and brave and be successful in Scotland with Celtic, even though, deep down, I was scared. So scared – it was frightening.

I had to travel alone. It was the first time I had ever been on a flight by myself, having always been with the team in the past. I was quite apprehensive, but it was also quite funny: I couldn't speak a word of English and my journey to Glasgow was via Brussels Airport. Thankfully, everything was OK, and with a combination of smiles and hand signals, I managed to negotiate my way through the various terminals and departure gates. I really think more people should learn to speak Bulgarian!

I cheered up when I eventually arrived in Glasgow later that day. Jamie Church, Celtic's chief of security, was waiting for me at the airport. He stood at the arrival gate holding up an A4 card with my name on it, and he also had a female interpreter with him, which was an enormous help. Word must have spread about my arrival as about 30 Celtic fans had turned up wanting my picture and autograph.

I was driven to a hotel in East Kilbride, and the whole experience seemed a bit surreal, but I remember being impressed with the buildings and general cleanliness of the city. I was still nervous. Although I had finally arrived at my new home, the most difficult period of my life was just about to begin.

Terry McDermott, who was on the Celtic coaching staff at that time, was waiting for me at my hotel. He was going to pick me up and drop me off at training every day for the first week. I then met up with another new signing from that summer, the Russian goalkeeper Dmitri Kharine. Soon, we all started to travel from the hotel to training together.

At the start, it was a nightmare. I don't think I ever ventured out of my room, and I didn't eat in the hotel. I ate at Celtic Park but had no idea what was on the menu as I couldn't understand English. I was too shy to go out and speak to people and spent most of my day speaking to friends and family back in Bulgaria on my mobile phone. I used it so much it got cut off after three days: it was a Bulgarian phone, and I'd used up all my credit.

I remember being really nervous on my first day at training, and I was scared to even try a pass any longer than two metres. A few of the boys had started to chat to me to make me feel welcome. I had an idea who a few of them were, because when I signed, I had done some research on the club to find out as much about Celtic as possible. I knew Eyal Berkovic had just signed, and Lubo Moravcik was also at the club. I just wanted to meet them and the rest of the boys, train with them and get the first few days out of the way. I was really nervous and knew I was going to be that way for a week or so.

On my first day with the team they sat me beside Lubo, Bobby Petta and Vidar Riseth in the corner of the dressing-room. The rest of the players all came to me and asked my name and how I was doing: just general chitchat to try and make me feel part of it. I now know what they were saying but didn't have a clue at the time, and I had no idea how to answer them. I just kept nodding – it was a very awkward situation. It was so frustrating not being able to communicate properly, and it also made me very lonely. Paul Lambert and Mark Burchill really made an extra effort, but even after a few weeks, I was barely beyond the 'yes' and 'no' stage.

Before I knew it, 15 August came around and it was time to make my debut against Dundee United at Tannadice. I was extremely nervous, and my apprehension wasn't helped by the fact we lost the game 2–1. I came on for Morten Wieghorst but didn't really get much of a chance to make an impression. There was no interpreter in the dressing-room to tell me how or where to play. It came down to basic football language and if I had to play right-back or left. It wasn't ideal.

John Barnes made changes to the team for our next league game, and it meant I started against Dundee at Dens Park. I played in the centre of midfield, and we won 2–1 thanks to a goal from Stéphane Mahé and a late winner from Henrik Larsson, after Lee Sharp had equalized for them.

I felt I really struggled in that match. The game was so fast, and I was well off the pace. I couldn't get a tackle in and couldn't seem to get close to the opposition. I hate to say it, but I was knackered after 20 minutes and knew there and then I had to improve my fitness. It was scary stuff. I knew it was going to be a long and difficult road ahead, but little did I know just how bad that first year would turn out to be. I had genuinely hoped for good times, but, instead, only trauma and heartache were in front of me, particularly during the first seven months. It was probably the worst time of my life.

2

The Day I Quit Celtic

When times were tough during my first few months in Glasgow, which they often were, it really got to me, and there were several occasions I thought about packing it all in and heading back to Bulgaria. One of the few positive things during those difficult first few months was that I was befriended by a guy from Glasgow called Brian Wilson. Brian took me under his wing and helped with the things that I was finding difficult to cope with.

At that time, I wasn't playing well, mainly because John Barnes was starting me at right-back, and I was struggling financially. After being in Glasgow for about two or three months, the pressures on and off the pitch all got too much for me, and I went through what I can only describe as a breakdown. One day, when I came home from training, it all just spilled out of me: the anger, the depression and the hurt.

I was raging, I was depressed and I didn't really have anyone to turn to. I remember lying on my living-room floor, beating the floorboards until my hands were too sore to take any more. The tears were streaming down my face. I was angry and alone. I had

had enough of Celtic. I had had enough of football. I had had enough of Glasgow. I just wanted to be back in Bulgaria with my family. It was as simple as that.

God only knows how, but I managed to get through that day and put my troubles to the back of my mind. After several hours thinking things over, I convinced myself it was all going to work out and that I would eventually enjoy playing for Celtic and living in Glasgow. I didn't know if I was just kidding myself in an attempt to cheer myself up, because for all I knew, it wouldn't be long before the depression reared its ugly head again.

About that time, I was given a holy candle by a friend over here who knew I was going through a really difficult period, and it sat on a shelf in my living room. I used to light it every night and say a prayer that things would get better. But, sadly, it wasn't getting any better – it actually began to get worse.

The bills were pouring in faster than my wallet could handle. I was still struggling to get by in day-to-day English, never mind reading and understanding letters and bills. Maintenance invoices were piling up: I owed about £300 for gas and around £200 for electricity. I also had a mobile phone bill of £6,000. It was a huge amount, but that was the price I had to pay for spending most of my time on the phone to my friends and family in Bulgaria, because I was so lonely and unhappy in Glasgow. I couldn't afford the bill and had no idea how to go about paying it. It was then that Brian stepped in and sorted it all out for me.

The saying in Scotland, I'm told, is 'Robbing Peter to pay Paul', and that was exactly what I had to do for the next six months to stabilise my financial situation. We spoke to all the various creditors, and they agreed on a system whereby I could start paying the bills in instalments. So I was paying £75 to one and £120 to another, although I had to fork out a lot more than that to the mobile phone company.

Still, it saved me the embarrassment of having to go to court if I had continued to ignore the red letters. It crossed my mind a few times that that's where I'd have been heading if Brian hadn't organised all of the repayment stuff for me. Or, at the very least, I would have had my electricity and phone cut off, and I'd have been blacklisted.

Despite all the bills, I was still managing to send some money back to Bulgaria to my family to make them as comfortable as possible. Apart from the fact I was a bit homesick, I didn't let them know too much about my problems. I didn't want them worrying for me and maybe feeling guilty about not being on hand to help. Also, I didn't want them to feel responsible for encouraging me to leave Bulgaria to play for Celtic.

Yes, it was a deeply depressing time, but throughout it all, I tried to see a funny side. And I did. You know, here I was, a Celtic player reportedly earning £15,000 a week, and I was paying off bills in this way. If I did earn that kind of money it wouldn't have been a problem, but I wasn't taking in anything like that amount – I wasn't even clearing a sixth of that. I understand that I was still making a fantastic living but my naivety regarding financial matters was getting me into trouble.

Fair enough, some people will probably think that it was my own fault for signing the contract in the first place and then not being able to handle my financial affairs properly, and I can, to an extent, understand that point of view, but it wasn't as simple as that.

I was genuinely unaware of bills coming through the door – council tax and the like – and nobody at Celtic told me that you had to go to a bank to pay them or set up a direct debit system. When I left Bulgaria to join Celtic there was very little, if anything, available on hire purchase, although now it is more common to use that system in my country. I couldn't believe it when I found out you can buy whatever you like, whether it's a car or a television, and walk away with it the same day without having to pay a penny. All you have to do is sign a piece of paper. It may be natural over here, but it's quite a dangerous thing, I think. Also, the cost of living over here is astronomical as compared with Bulgaria. When I looked at my wages on the contract that I signed on day one for

You Can Call Me Stan

Celtic, I was looking at it from what they would be like in Bulgaria, a country where the national average monthly wage packet is around £70. But this was Scotland, and I had no idea how far my monthly salary would stretch.

The estate agent Celtic used to find me somewhere to live put me into a rented four-bedroom flat in the west end of Glasgow that I couldn't afford. It was far too big for me, and I only used the living room. I bought myself a sofa bed and sat on that to watch television or listen to music. Or use my mobile phone. When it was time to go to sleep I made it into a bed. So, in the time I lived in that flat I hardly set foot in one of the bedrooms, never mind get use out of all four of them.

The flat had all the up-to-date accessories, but I didn't know how to work the top-of-the-range washing machine, and I ended up washing my clothes by hand at the sink in the kitchen! The cooker was also fantastic, and the oven was big enough to cook enough food to feed the entire Jock Stein Stand, but I couldn't use it. I was a bit worried that I might end up setting the place on fire, and I wasn't sure if I was insured for that or not.

I have a good appetite and hate going without food, but rather than use my amazing cooker, I ended up making all my meals in the microwave – it was simple and safe but was absolutely no good for my waistline. My diet was terrible, and I knew I was starting to put on weight.

That, though, was the least of my worries. Living in that luxury flat nearly finished me financially. I even had a cleaner coming in twice a week. I thought it was part of the service of the flat, and I couldn't believe it when a monthly bill for £400 dropped through the letterbox. If I had known that, I would have turned the cleaner away on day one. I didn't have money to burn on luxuries – especially as I was only using one room! But I couldn't speak English so I couldn't ask the cleaner what she was doing and who had sent her to my flat. I just let her get on with it. To be honest, I think some people were taking advantage of the fact I couldn't speak the language.

Again, cynics will say it's my own fault for not establishing everything from day one, and I accept that I have to take some responsibility. But remember, I was just 19 years old when I arrived here and needed help, support and guidance. I don't want to be over-critical of Celtic, but I don't believe I had nearly enough guidance from the club, and it still annoys me to this day when I think of how I was left to get on with it without proper help.

When a young man arrives in a new country, especially one you have invested millions of pounds in, shouldn't everything possible be done to make sure he is an asset to the company? If that's not the case then the investment is in danger of becoming a waste of money. That's what almost happened to me. I'd like to think that in the future, if Celtic sign any players in a similar situation, the football club will have learned from their experience with me. I totally accept mistakes can happen and allowances have to be made, but you must learn from your mistakes. The people running Celtic Football Club now are different from when I joined, and I'm pleased to say that things are better for the new signings. The support network is much more professional, particularly for players arriving from foreign countries.

I noticed that when Mikel Arteta and Jean-Alain Boumsong joined Rangers they brought members of their immediate family to live with them in Glasgow and it helped them settle. What a smart move. I would have loved to be in a position to do that, but it wasn't possible.

I remember that when Rafael Scheidt joined the club in January 2000 he had the club coordinator Celine Wilson on hand 24 hours a day to help sort out the things you need to do when you move to a new country. If he was ever unsure about anything, he could call her up at any time to seek her advice or ask her to sort out the problem. The same woman was at the club when I joined but didn't speak Bulgarian. I think she spoke French and Spanish, but that was of no use to me.

I spoke to Rafael about the problems of settling, but he didn't really have off-the-field things to worry about as he had Celine and a much better wage packet than me. He had all of that other stuff taken care of and just had to concentrate on playing football. I was a little jealous of that and angry I hadn't been looked after in the same way.

However, his wage packet and Celine couldn't do anything to help Rafael when he was out on the pitch playing for Celtic. Rafael sampled the difficulty of life playing for one half of the Old Firm, and he was under pressure after a few games. He struggled to settle, and I think the price tag of around £5 million took its toll on him. Everyone was expecting a typical Brazilian – classy and oozing confidence – but, sadly, it didn't turn out that way.

I remember when he was receiving stick from the media and a few of our fans, I went out for a meal with him, Bobby Petta and Olivier Tebily. We dined in a lovely restaurant in Glasgow. It was a decent night, and I think the fact we were all new signings and all not doing particularly well gave us a lot in common. It was great for us because we managed to get a few things off our chest and help each other cope with the problems we were experiencing. However, when we left the restaurant we were no sooner on the pavement than a member of the public started shouting abuse at Rafael. He knew the comments weren't exactly favourable but couldn't quite make them out properly. He asked us if we understood what the guy was saying, but we just said it wasn't anything too bad and told him to get into the car. If we had told him the truth and said that the guy was slaughtering him, I think he'd have been in the mood to challenge the guy, and it could have turned nasty.

I could understand most of what was being said that night, but there was a time when my English was non-existent, and I couldn't hold a minute of conversation with anyone. When someone spoke to me I just nodded, but I didn't have a clue what they were saying.

On the park it was worse. I remember picking up a stomach injury during an Old Firm match that made it difficult for me to breathe. I lay on the ground for treatment, but when our physio Brian Scott came on, I couldn't explain to him what was wrong. It was at that point that he and Brian Wilson decided to take me aside and teach me how to say 'leg', 'arm', 'knee' and 'head'.

There was also one time that I had an awful toothache, caused by a painful abscess on my gum. I was in agony. I was frustrated that I couldn't explain that I needed to see a dentist, and it took longer than it should have to sort the problem out. The delay in receiving treatment meant I had to get a tooth out.

I was terrified about going to the dentist. In Bulgaria they don't use a needle to numb the gum, they just get right in there and get on with it. I thought it would be the same over here, but, thankfully, it didn't turn out to be nearly as painful an experience as I thought it was going to be.

Brian Wilson was a help with the language, which was just as well because Celtic had organised English lessons for me at Hamilton College. I didn't drive at the time and it was an awkward place to get to. After my first night-time lesson, I didn't get home until quite late, having had to use public transport, so I decided it wasn't worth it. In all honesty, I thought it would have been better for Celtic to organise the language teacher to come to Parkhead or to my house. When I first arrived from Bulgaria, a student from my homeland called Mitko Petrov was studying in Edinburgh, and he helped translate for the first few days but didn't have the time to stay with me on a full-time basis.

But Brian was there to help. He worked at Celtic Park, and that was where I met him. He gave me a lift one day from the ground to my hotel in East Kilbride, and during that 20-minute journey we struck up a friendship, which was funny because neither of us could understand a word the other was saying. He has a broad Glaswegian accent but we gradually made ourselves understood, mainly by making signs rather than talking.

Our friendship just blossomed, and I can say for sure that my life in Glasgow would have been a lot less happy had Brian not been there for me. In fact, I probably would have left the club, had it not been for him persuading me to stay and stick it out. He is my Scottish father. In the morning when he drove me into training, he'd teach me essential football talk like 'man-on', 'time' and 'keeper's ball', as I was struggling with even the basic stuff.

Another way I improved my English was to go to the movies every other night. Honestly, I was there that often, I must have been a real boost to the profit margin at the Glasgow Quayside! My favourite movies were *Ace Ventura*, *51st State* and *Ronin*. I think I watched *51st State* about four times in a fortnight. Robert Carlyle is a fantastic actor, and I'm not just saying that because he's Scottish.

The cinema was a great help to me. I had to concentrate hard to try and understand the movie and what was going on. It was a great way of really getting to grips with how English is spoken, and I could have a laugh at the same time. I found that much better than sitting in a classroom and learning the language in a cold, no-nonsense fashion.

As my English improved it allowed me to go into Parkhead in the morning and join in the fun, although it wasn't exactly a bundle of laughs during John Barnes's time. There's no denying that there were a couple of problems in the dressing-room and some players just didn't see eye to eye. When you think that we had quality players like Eyal Berkovic, Henrik Larsson, Paul Lambert, Lubo Moravcik and Mark Viduka we shouldn't have been losing domestic games. But we were poor, and I can only think that it was down to the team spirit not being right, rather than the players not having the ability. A team that is not prepared to give 110 per cent for each other and the manager will always have problems. John Barnes just didn't seem to possess the authority to go in and sort it all out. Maybe he wasn't even fully aware of how bad it was – I don't know.

Part of his problem was that he had his favourites and didn't treat everyone the same. If he left a player out of the side he would rarely, if ever, explain why, and that made a lot of players resent him. I wasn't fully aware of the extent of the problems as my English was poor, and I couldn't understand what was being said by the players in the dressing-room and on the training pitch.

It was really important to learn English as I was feeling left out of a lot of things. Mark Burchill really made an effort to help, and we became great friends. We still are. In fact, I'm sure it was Burchie that gave me my nickname, Stan. He thought Stiliyan was too much of a mouthful and that Stan was much easier. The Celtic fans also call me that now, and the name has stuck. Even people in Bulgaria call me Stan, and I think it is quite a nice name.

Because we were such good mates, I was desperately sorry to see Burchie leave Celtic to go to Portsmouth – he's a really good striker, and I hope he goes on to have a successful career. However, I got the impression that not every player in the dressing-room felt the same way about me as Burchie did. In the early months, when my form was poor and I was having loads of problems, I could sense a couple of my teammates questioning what I was doing at the club. It seemed they'd made their minds up about me and thought that Celtic had wasted £2 million. I got the impression that the popular opinion was that I didn't deserve to be anywhere near a first-team jersey. I also knew that the supporters hadn't accepted me at that time, and I reckon few of them believed that I would be an asset to the club. Believe me, it wasn't a nice feeling and became another reason why I felt that I should walk away and move back to Bulgaria.

The loneliness was hurting me, and I felt completely out of it. I'm a guy that loves training, and, from an early age, I've always stayed behind to work on things on the training pitch or put in an extra session in the gym. However, at that time, training couldn't finish quickly enough, and I was so happy to get out the door. It reached the stage that the only thing I looked forward to was finishing training and heading up to a friend's burger van in the north of Glasgow. There I was, Celtic's £2 million midfielder, eating hamburgers and chicken burgers in a van. I was starting to pile on weight again, but I couldn't help it: I was comfort eating.

When I wasn't eating burgers, I loved getting behind the counter and serving the punters. It was great fun, and the people were so nice and friendly, typical Glaswegians. Again, I didn't have a clue what they were saying. The only thing harder to understand than a Glaswegian accent is a drunken man with a Glaswegian accent. And, believe me, I served a few of them. I remember one guy turned up who, by the look of him, had been out enjoying himself in the pub. He ordered some food, and I could see the confused look on his face as he looked up at me as if he was saying to himself, 'That looks like Stiliyan Petrov but it *can't* be, not a Celtic player serving in a burger van.' The funny thing was, the guy must have thought he was much more drunk than he actually was.

The other happy memory that sticks in my mind during the bad times was the night I won the lottery. Brian put two lines on one Saturday afternoon in November, and we promised each other that we'd share the money if we were lucky enough to win. Well, five of our six numbers came up on one of the lines and we scooped £2,000. I was so happy to pick up half of that. Honestly, I felt like I had won a million pounds, even though I still had another £999,000 to make up. I couldn't have cared less, even though we were just one correct number away from winning about £7 million.

I decided to splash out, and for the first time since I had arrived in Glasgow I had a few pounds to spend on some new clothes. I had been wearing the same gear since arriving from Bulgaria, and it was time to bring myself up to date with the Western world by buying some trendy gear. When I left a clothes shop in Glasgow's West End with four or five bags full of stuff, I felt like I should be parading up and down a Milan catwalk.

But despite Brian's help and the fact that I finally had some money to spend, it wasn't long before the loneliness and depression came back. I'd had enough, and I wanted to go home. Late one night, I packed my case and prepared to go back to Bulgaria.

The crisis point came after a midweek game in November 1999 against Motherwell at Celtic Park. We lost 1–0, and I was at fault for the goal. Yet again, I was playing at right-back, and Kevin Twaddle skinned me to score the winner. The boos were ringing around Celtic Park, and I felt it was all down to me. It was the lowest point of my footballing life, and it brought everything to a head.

The Day I Quit Celtic

When I was driving home with Brian that night I just let everything out. I'll never forget that dark, depressing night as we made our way along London Road. I told him that I had made a big, big mistake in joining Celtic. We drove around for a while, and Brian tried to get me to see the positive side of being at Parkhead. However, in my opinion, the bad far outweighed the good, and there was no way I was going to change my mind.

Brian dropped me off at my flat – by this time I had found more suitable accommodation on the south side of the city – and told me not to do anything rash. He said that I should sleep on it and that everything would be better in the morning, but I am headstrong and was determined to leave. As soon as I got into the flat I broke down in tears. The walls were closing in on me, and I just felt trapped. I hated my life in Glasgow with Celtic and wanted out of it.

I hadn't improved 1 per cent since I had joined Celtic. If anything, I had gone backwards. It wasn't the way it was supposed to have been. I was also angry with myself for signing the contract with the club and leaving behind my happy life in Bulgaria. I suppose that if I had been married to Paulina at the time it would have been fine. Paulina is a calming influence and just having her around would have made life so much more bearable. But she was back in Bulgaria studying and had her university course to complete.

That night I packed my case and phoned my parents to tell them I was coming home for good. They were upset and told me that I shouldn't rush into things, but I knew they would stand by my decision, even if they didn't wholeheartedly agree with it.

All sorts of things were running through my head as I sat on a chair in my living room in the dark. When was I going to tell Celtic? What was I going to say to them? What was I going to tell everyone? Would I ever play professional football again? That last question really got me going. I knew that if I just walked out on Celtic I was leaving myself open to all sorts of punishment. The club would try and get me back, but if I refused, they wouldn't just let me go. I had cost them a lot of cash, and they had every right to fight to get their money's worth or their investment back by transferring me.

Then it crossed my mind that FIFA would have to become involved. I could end up with my name being mud and might even face the prospect of being banned from football. But I was ready for that; that's how sickened I felt. I had a plan worked out. I would just go back to Bulgaria and get a job in my friend's sports shop or work as a waiter in another friend's restaurant. Anything would have been better than what I was doing in Glasgow. So my bag was packed.

I phoned Brian first thing in the morning and asked him to take me to the airport. I had phoned an airline to ask about flight times, and I had booked my tickets. Brian arrived and we had a good chat about what I was about to do. He told me that I was making a huge mistake, but I didn't listen. By the time we arrived at Glasgow Airport, our discussion had developed into a full-scale shouting match, but I was still ready to say my farewells, never to return. I was walking into the terminal with Brian when, all of a sudden, something hit me. I really don't know what it was, but I just stopped walking and said to Brian that I had changed my mind and that he should take me to Celtic Park for training.

Honestly, I can't put my finger on one single thing that made me change my mind. It must have been a combination of things, such as letting myself down and earning a bad reputation. I might also have jeopardised any future moves for Bulgarian footballers to Scotland by walking out. But, above all, I didn't want to be remembered as a failure. The fans had been fairly tolerant of me, and I had to repay them by helping Celtic to win the league again and in the process do myself proper justice. They were patient enough with me, I just wasn't being patient enough with myself.

I told Brian that I had changed my mind, and the smile on his face convinced me even more that I was doing the right thing. He drove me to Parkhead, and I walked through the glass doors at the stadium that morning as if nothing had happened. I never told anyone that an hour earlier I was only a few steps away from walking out on Celtic.

3

My Favourite Team –
Me, Paulina and
Stiliyan, jun.

Having come from a solid upbringing, I always felt that it was important to have the same for my own family when I was older. That's why I consider myself lucky to have met Paulina Serafimova. She is now my wife, and we have been blessed with a beautiful son whom we named Stiliyan.

Since the day we met in 1999, Paulina has always been there for me, and how we met is an interesting story. I played in an away game for Bulgaria against Ukraine shortly after signing for Celtic. Georgi Bachev, one of my international teammates, asked me if I wanted to join a few of the boys for a drink when we returned to Sofia. I was single and happy to join them.

When we were out, Paulina and a friend of hers were at the same restaurant as us. I was introduced to the pal, and we spoke for about half an hour. Then I was introduced to Paulina and we spoke for a while. There was definitely some kind of spark between us, and I was keen to meet her again. I was too shy to tell her that I wanted to see her again, but I noticed that Paulina had given her mobile phone number to her friend to pass on to me. I spoke to Paulina again the next day, after I'd built up the courage to phone her. You've no idea how nervous I was before making that follow-up call. It was scarier than an Old Firm game!

I was soon back in Glasgow, and our relationship was conducted over the phone for the next few months. It was almost a month after our first date before we met again face to face, but we were on the phone to each other every day. We were quite shy when we met again back in Bulgaria. We had a nice meal together, and I wanted to kiss her before the night was over but was too bashful to try.

The phone conversations continued, and it was another month before we met again. I knew that I wanted our relationship to become more serious. Less than six months after meeting her, I asked Paulina if she would consider moving to Glasgow to live with me. I told her that Scotland was a nice country and that Glasgow was a beautiful city. I was lonely and wanted her with me.

It was a big decision for her to make because she was at university, and I was asking her to give up everything for me: her family, friends and education. I was delighted when she agreed to leave Sofia because I had to be with her more often than just once every two months for it to be a proper relationship. Paulina agreed to give up her full-time economics course to move to Glasgow, and I felt a little guilty because she had worked so hard to get a place at Sofia University. The fact that she gave up her studies in Bulgaria to come to Scotland shows how much Paulina loves me, but I was delighted that she continued her course in Scotland, graduating in 2005. If she hadn't moved to Glasgow when she did, I might well have chucked it and moved back to Bulgaria to be with her.

The first few months in Glasgow were difficult for her. It was easier once she picked up English, and her second language is no problem for her now. She didn't go out much for the first seven or eight months, and I had a lot of sympathy for her. It was difficult for me, but I was determined to make her happy. Paulina is a great character and a great person. She is a smart girl and makes good decisions for our family. I trust her and love her.

We had been together for about 18 months when I decided to ask her to marry me. We had spoken about it one night when we were out having dinner in Glasgow at our good friend Milan Cvetkovc's restaurant. Then one day after training, I came home and decided that would be the day. I already had an engagement ring and proposed to her at our flat on the south side of Glasgow. The ring was a little big for Paulina's finger but didn't need too much adjustment. She accepted my proposal and we are now very settled and love our lives in Scotland. We really have no desire to leave and move to another country. We are happy as a family in Glasgow and don't envisage that changing.

In the past, there has been talk about clubs from Italy, Spain and Germany being interested in me and it's flattering, but I'm not sure I would want to uproot and start a new life elsewhere. It was tough for me when I first moved to Scotland from Bulgaria, and the thought of switching to another country to learn another new language and integrate into that particular country's culture is not something that appeals to me. It honestly doesn't.

And it's not just about me: I now have a family to think about. When you move to one of the major countries in Europe you could end up being away for between 90 and 100 days a year, preparing for matches or travelling to away games. That's not ideal when you have a young family, and the last thing I want is for Paulina to be lonely and miserable. I would also hate not being there to see huge chunks of young Stiliyan's growing up. If your family and home life is not settled, it doesn't help your career as a professional footballer. At this moment in time, Celtic give me and my family everything we need.

When young Stiliyan arrived, we were so happy. I remember when we were on holiday in Cancun, Mexico, in the summer of 2002, we spoke about having kids, and Paulina fell pregnant almost immediately afterwards. On our return to Bulgaria after the holiday, she felt tired and sick, and, out of curiosity, we decided to get a pregnancy kit. She took the test one night, and then again the following morning, and it was confirmed. We were both delighted. Paulina asked me to keep our news a secret because she was just five weeks gone, but I couldn't keep my mouth shut, and after she went to see the doctor and he confirmed it, I told everyone. I couldn't keep it quiet. I was so happy and proud.

The nine months of Paulina's pregnancy seemed to fly in. Before we knew it, Paulina was having contractions and we were rushing to hospital. I asked the doctor if I could sleep there until the baby was born because I didn't want to return home and have a mad rush to get back in when the baby was due. I managed to get a room in the hospital, and I slept on a sofa bed.

The birth was quite straightforward – well, it looked that way to me! Young Stiliyan was born, almost nine months to the day after Paulina fell pregnant, on 11 February 2003 in the Queen Mother's Hospital in Glasgow. He's a great kid who can speak English and Bulgarian, and he also qualifies to play for both Scotland and Bulgaria should he decide to follow in his father's footsteps.

I was delighted my mother and Paulina's mother Rumyana were in Glasgow the day Stiliyan was born. We invited them to attend the birth but they were too nervous! They stayed at our house for the first couple of months, and their experience and advice were invaluable to us.

In Bulgaria, some people like to take a baby's umbilical cord and place it somewhere they think will bring luck to their child. When Stiliyan's cord came off I took it to Celtic Park and threw it onto the turf inside the 18-yard box at the Celtic End. I would love to see him go on and play for Celtic, and that's why I decided to throw it there.

Our young family loves its life in Scotland, and much of the reason for that is down to the way the Scottish people have accepted us. Brian Wilson, in particular, has made us feel welcome and helped us to settle here. I am so grateful that he gave me a lift home on the day that we first met, otherwise we might not be friends now. That afternoon, the boys had been going out for a 'bonding session' together, but I couldn't speak English and didn't really fancy it. In saying that, none of the players at that time made any effort to get me to come out with them and feel a part of it. On the way back to my hotel, I discovered that Brian is a really funny guy, with a typical Glasgow sense of humour, and our friendship has grown and grown since that first meeting.

I have so much time for Brian. His knowledge of Celtic and the Glasgow area has been invaluable to us. I know that he will be a friend for life. He and his family have sacrificed so much for us. When I thought that we were going to lose him after he suffered a heart attack on 14 December 2002 I was devastated. It was a Saturday night, and Martin O'Neill gave me permission to leave the team hotel to go and see him at the Western Hospital. It was frightening to see him lying motionless in a hospital bed. Thankfully, he fought back from it and made a full recovery. He does take life much easier now. His only vice appears to be drinking cans of Coke: he manages to get through about 20 a day!

Brian has always encouraged me to stay with Celtic, and they really have a lot to thank him for. In the past, I've had chances to manoeuvre my way out of the club, but I've never attempted to use a situation to my advantage to make more money. I won't mention specific names or specific clubs, but I can recall being approached at least three times to see if I fancied leaving Celtic. One of the potential moves, which came about during the 2004–05 season, would have earned me more than double the salary I was on at Celtic. But my answer in such circumstances has always been the same. I have told any potential suitor to go and make their approaches through the proper channels. Go and ask Celtic if I am for sale, and if a transfer fee can be agreed and the club gives me permission to talk, I will always show my manners and listen to what they have to say.

People will think what they like about me, but I believe I am an honest man. I am also very shy and quiet. I am loyal to my friends and teammates. I keep things to myself – things that I know others would speak of or complain about. During my time at Celtic I could perhaps have been pushier about a few issues, but I have always maintained my professionalism. I feel that I have served the club well.

I am now in my seventh season at Parkhead, which makes me the longest-serving player on the books. I've seen managers come and go, and I've seen many teammates leave the club. I have counted them up and – unless I'm mistaken – at the time of writing, 41 of my teammates have left. Quite unbelievable. They are, in no particular order: Dmitri Kharine, Rab Douglas, Jonathan Gould, Stewart Kerr, Magnus Hedman, Steve Guppy, Ramon Vega, Oliver Tebily, Javier Sanchez-Broto, Eyal Berkovic, Bobby Petta, Rafael Scheidt, Vidar Riseth, Regi Blinker, Henrik Larsson, Johan Mjällby, Alan Stubbs, Mark Viduka, Tommy Johnson, Mark Burchill, Harald Brattbakk, Craig Burley, Paul Lambert, Jackie McNamara, David Fernandez, Momo Sylla, Joos Valgaeren, Morten Wieghorst, Colin Healy, Liam Miller, Stephen Crainey, Jamie Smith, Juninho, Henri Camara, Lubo Moravcik, Ulrik Laursen, Tom Boyd, Craig Bellamy, Stéphane Henchoz, Michael Gray and Ian Wright.

Many of these guys have helped me become a successful Celtic player, and one of the proudest nights of my life came in May 2005 when I was voted the Player of the Year by my teammates and also won the fans' award as well. It was a privilege to pick up those two special honours.

I never thought that I would ever become the player in the dressing-room with the longest service. As a result, I feel a responsibility to the club and my teammates. I want to make sure players settle and always try to make every guy feel welcome, particularly when they come from abroad. I've tried to mak Maciej Zurawski and Artur Boruc settle in off the park by showing them good places to eat and shop and any small things to make life in Glasgow more enjoyable because I know how difficult it is to come to terms with everything when you move here from another country.

My contract with Celtic runs until the summer of 2007. If I see it through until then, that will take me to eight years' service. I genuinely hope I'm with Celtic for longer than that. When my contract expires I will be 28, and, at that age, I will be making the most important decision of my career. I have signed deals in the past that I have not been 100 per cent happy with. However, I have agreed to them because I'd had enough of negotiations and just wanted the decision to be over and done with. That is entirely my own fault. But in the future I will not agree to anything that's not absolutely 100 per cent right for me and my family. When the contract negotiations come about, I'll be approaching what should be the best three or four years of my career, and there will be no way back after that. I don't want to be sitting in my house when I'm 40 regretting the decision I made when I was 28.

It will not be all about money, although I can't deny I'd expect the club to offer me a package befitting my status as a senior player who has given fine service and will be at the peak years of his career. Just as important – if not more important – will be the direction the club is going. If Celtic make me feel wanted and have the right ambition, I will be more than happy to stay, but we must always be aiming to move forward. Aiming to bring in the best available players. Aiming to be a club that can make an impact in the Champions League. If I can see it with my own two eyes and the people in power at Celtic also assure me, I will stay. I hope we can reach an agreement, and I hope it can be settled long before my contract expires in June 2007.

Of course, it's well known that there has been interest in me from different clubs, and it could well be that in the future I will be presented with offers from teams in England and Spain. It is my duty to consider everything put in front of me. I owe that much to myself and my family. Right now, though, Celtic remain in the driving seat, and they showed their commitment to me when they rejected a bid of around £3.5 million from Fulham in August 2005. I was flattered by the interest from the London side and equally flattered that Celtic decided to keep me.

4

Growing Up in Bulgaria

I'm lucky to come from a loving and caring family that would do anything for one another. My father Aliosha, mother Svetla, younger brother Ivan and I all have a strong relationship. It was just as well we cared for one another so deeply because there were difficult times. We really had to dig deep for each other. If the love hadn't been there, I don't how we would have survived the stressful periods. Bulgaria is not a wealthy country and many families struggle to make ends meet.

I was born in Montana on 5 July 1979. We lived on the fourth floor of a five-storey block of flats, in one of the oldest buildings in the town. It was a normal flat with a living room, kitchen, bathroom and two bedrooms. My parents continued to live there until recently but now have a newer, more modern apartment.

Montana is a nice little place with a population of about 65,000. It's a town where just about every face is a familiar one and most people know each other. It is very quiet with only a handful of main roads, a few restaurants and cafés, some shops and a small hospital. It is a long way off from being like a place such as Glasgow: we don't have any designer clothes shops for a start.

Bulgaria isn't fully Westernised yet. The differences between Scotland and home can be quite stark sometimes. However, Bulgarian food is very good, and eating out is inexpensive. I remember going out for a meal with five friends in Sofia recently, and we had three courses each and some drinks. The bill for the night was no more than £25.

Bulgaria is a place I love, and I've never heard anyone who's visited my country say bad things about it. I'm so happy that it is becoming more and more popular with British people as a holiday destination. The fact there are now direct flights from Glasgow to Bulgaria is fantastic.

But, like all countries, it does have its negative aspects. When I was younger I remember that my parents sometimes didn't receive their wages on time, and it meant we struggled to pay the electricity and water bills. The delays were most often down to the fact that there's no proper system over there like the one we have here, whereby salaries are credited to bank accounts at the end of each month. In Bulgaria it is more or less cash in hand, and sometimes employers don't have enough money, so employees have to go without. That kind of thing can happen two or three months on the trot, and it can be difficult to live on a day-to-day basis under such trying circumstances. It happened to my mother, and she has what's regarded as a decent job as a schoolteacher.

If the wages were late, we might not have any meat on the table for a couple of weeks. I love my food and my favourite dish is my mum's homemade chicken and potatoes. It's her speciality, and I'm not exaggerating when I say that I wanted to have it every day when I was a kid! Even the smell of it made me hungry. To go without was hard.

In saying that, things are not nearly as bad as they were ten years ago and they are definitely improving in the country. There is more of a structure to the way Bulgaria operates now, and everyone is thankful for that. There's still a lot of work to be done, but steps are being taken, and things are now done in a more professional manner.

When times were tough we all chipped in to keep our spirits up, and my grandparents would also contribute as much as possible. I will never forget my roots and never forget the tough times – that is why I wake up every day in Glasgow and appreciate all the good things I have in life. Now that I'm a footballer and earn good money, I can help my family and send them back cash to make sure they are as comfortable as possible. Despite this, they still want to lead the same life they always have; they don't want the money to change their lives too much. My family still lives in Montana, and I admire the fact they've continued to live there and try to lead the same way of life.

One thing my cash has managed to bring is a new Volkswagen Golf for my dad, which he was delighted to accept in place of his old Lada. I also helped him financially to start his own transport company, and he enjoys the responsibility, challenge and pressure of maintaining a successful business.

Don't get me wrong, we still had a television and a video when I was a boy; it wasn't like we lived in the Dark Ages. But there are still things we have to change in my country. For example, without warning they sometimes turn off the electricity for two hours. This can cause real problems, especially in the winter when the houses go cold without their electrical heating. It often meant that at night the four of us would have to sleep in my parents' bed to make sure we stayed warm.

I still enjoy going back to Montana to see my friends, and we regularly keep in touch. I love going back to see them three or four times a year and having a party. I like to speak to the neighbours in my parents' building and see how everyone is getting on. My friends also like to visit me when I'm home, and my parents' house usually ends up as busy as Sauchiehall Street with people constantly knocking on the door to see how I am. One time, as word got out that I was home, we had a queue outside the door: kids from all over the place had come to see me. I signed their T-shirts and football jerseys and they had their photographs taken with me. I'm happy to do things like that – it is never a problem for me to help brighten up the day for other people, especially young kids. The first time I returned home, I took a suitcase full of Celtic tops – I think I had 50 of them – and gave them to family, friends and neighbours. I wanted as many people as possible to wear the green and white hoops, and I was proud to give them the jersey.

Going home to Montana is also good because it gives me the chance to catch up with Ivan and spend some time with him. He is three years younger than me, and we are still really close. I love him so much and will help him in every way I can. When we were growing up we shared a bedroom. We often joined our two single beds together so that we were close to each other, and we would have a laugh and giggle before going to sleep. Despite the fun we used to have when we were young, as we got older Ivan asked for the beds to be moved apart. Apparently, I used to move around too much at night, steal the covers from him and snore my head off! Apart from that, I was OK to share a bed with!

We also used to fight like cat and dog. Some of the battles we had still send shivers down my spine. Because I was the big brother, I used to think I was right all the time, and Ivan couldn't accept that. In retaliation, he would throw stones at me, and he cut my head open five or six times when he managed to hit me. I needed a couple of stitches once, but most of the time it was just an ice pack and a lie down. And he is still at it. I am a more disciplined person and can accept things, even if I don't agree with them. For instance, I accepted life in the army and obeyed the rules, but Ivan couldn't do that. He can go crazy sometimes if he doesn't agree with something, and I know he had fights with the officers in the army to make a point about certain aspects of camp life he wasn't happy with.

He has completed his army service now and would like to make a career in football. He is a really good player, and I hope he makes it. He has played for FC Academic in the Bulgarian first division, but I have sympathy for him because he is always being compared with me, and that's not right. People say he should be able to handle such pressure, but I didn't have those pressures when I started out on my career. He is Ivan; I am Stiliyan. We are brothers but we are not the same person.

In saying all that, he is a very caring person and often worries about me. He gets really annoyed with me if I go more than two days without phoning home to speak to him or my parents. He ends up out of his mind with worry, and I hate putting him through that torture. He gives me a hard time for not keeping in touch, and now I make sure I contact my family every day. When I broke my leg he cried down the phone and told me he loved me. He had dozens of questions that he wanted me to answer about the leg break I suffered in a game against St Johnstone and what the consequences might be, but I didn't know what the answers were, and that made him even more upset.

Ivan also has a good sense of humour, and when I scored my four free-kicks in a row against Dundee, Juventus, Aberdeen and Rangers in 2001, he phoned me up to ask me how much money it had cost me to bribe the goalkeepers! That keeps me on my toes, and all of the family are the same.

I have other family in Montana, although both of my dad's parents are dead. His mother was called Stiliyana, and I was named after her. I never met her as she died in a car crash in March 1965. She was driving with her friend over a bridge in Montana and lost control of the car as she swerved to avoid an oncoming vehicle. It was a wet night, and there was nothing she could do as the car crashed through the barrier and ended up in the river. Her friend was also killed.

My father took me to the bridge to show me where she died, and it was a really touching moment. It was almost as if I could feel her presence and that she was glad I had paid my respects to her at the place where she spent the last few seconds of her life. I have been back a few times and have found myself there a couple of times to talk to her if I have had anything on my mind that might be troubling me.

You Can Call Me Stan

The feelings that I had for my grandfather are the same as those that I had for my grandmother. I miss him terribly. He was great with me about my football and used to give me plenty of encouragement. He took me to see FC Montana play when I was a boy, and I loved those days out at the football that we spent together. Just me and him – it was fantastic.

He worked at the Montana football stadium, and he was so proud of me when I played for them. He used to love his work, doing all sorts of things for the club, as well as watching them play. When I signed for them as a 16 year old they were in the top division, and my first wage as a footballer was £7 a month. After one year at Montana, CSKA Sofia signed me after they had heard good reports, and I suppose I must have played well against them at some point. So, I joined them when I was 17 and stayed for two years until Celtic came in for me.

CSKA paid me almost £5,000 a year. It was an excellent wage for a young boy in Bulgaria, and I was considered to be well off. However, the bonus system at the club was inconsistent to say the least. The club would offer us different bonuses before every game because we didn't have a written bonus structure in our contracts. Basically, the way it worked was that our bonus system depended on who the club president was and what kind of mood he was in! If he was in a good mood, we'd agree a generous bonus before the game. But sometimes we would go two or three wins without any bonus, and if we lost a game the president would come into the dressing-room and tell us we had been fined the three win bonuses we had already earned for losing that game. We couldn't argue, even though we were all unhappy with the decision.

The club would also stagger payments. I remember that we won a game in the UEFA Cup against Servette, and it took CSKA four months to pay the win bonus of about £1,500 per man. It meant the players had to go around tapping each other for money. Sometimes we'd go weeks on end without pay, and the wages were always paid in cash, never into a bank account.

The club would also get money back from you in other ways. I remember being fined £20 for eating my dinner too quickly at the team hotel the night before a game. However, I'd never complain too much about life as a footballer. It all started for me at Montana, and that football club has a special place in my heart. Whenever I visit the stadium, I always remember my grandfather.

When I was a teenager, I remember leaving Montana Stadium after training one day and making my way home. My grandfather had left the house to go and buy some bread. Outside a shop I noticed a big crowd had gathered, and when I got home my mother told me that my grandfather had collapsed in the street as the result of a heart attack and died. I knew as soon as she told me the news that the big crowd I had just passed on the street was gathered around my grandfather. My father started to cry, and that was the first time in my life I'd ever seen him break down in tears. A lot of bad things happened to my father in his life but he never let me or my brother see it get to him. This was different, though. He had just lost his father, and, understandably, it was all too much.

My grandfather was a great man and made me feel very special. At Christmas time, from when I was about four years old until I was about eight, he would dress up as Santa and we would have to write a poem to Father Christmas to make sure we received our presents. I didn't know it was my grandfather dressed up as Santa, and I thought it was a real person. One year my brother recognised him but didn't want to say anything in case my grandfather didn't bring him a present. We were lucky enough to always receive nice presents, such as new training shoes, and I was always happy with the gifts.

In Bulgaria, we celebrate Christmas on 24 December and exchange presents at night after we have had our meal. A traditional Christmas dinner is usually a six-course vegetarian meal with a few glasses of wine. Up until 1989, when communist rule ended after the national assembly voted for political change, some people didn't celebrate Christmas. I think things have improved in Bulgaria since the move to democracy, but I know that plenty of older people preferred communist rule, as everyone was more or less the same. Now they think the rich are getting richer and the poor are getting poorer.

In Bulgaria, New Year is more special than Christmas. We all have a good time, and there is usually a massive fireworks display. I don't know when I'll next be in Montana for the New Year fireworks display. It's those little aspects of life that I miss about home, and I'm looking forward to experiencing them again when I stop playing football. Don't get me wrong, I love my job, but you have to sacrifice a lot of time with your family, and I find that difficult.

It was my family that encouraged me to become a footballer and taught me from an early age the little things that have helped me to reach the stage that I'm at today. My mum and dad were also strict with me on certain things when I was growing up. For example, I was 15 before I was ever in a junior nightclub, and, even then, I still had to be back in the house by 10 p.m.

I was 17 when I sampled alcohol for the first time – I drank vodka in a nightclub with some friends, but it tasted horrible. It was later that year that I got drunk for the first time. It happened after I was dropped from the CSKA side for four or five games. The other boys encouraged me to drown my sorrows, and I ended up being sick for days. In a way, though, it turned out to be a blessing in disguise, because after that incident I've never really taken to drink in the same way again. I enjoy going out for a few refreshments but never drink to get drunk. I hate getting hangovers, and there's nothing worse than having a splitting headache because of alcohol. It also hampers your performance in training, and I like my body to be in the best condition possible.

I have worked hard during my life to make it as a footballer, and I'm proud it has worked out so well. It has been a long and difficult road, and there is still plenty of hard work ahead. My mum often tells me that I had a ball and from the age of 18 months loved to pick it up and throw it about. I then progressed to kicking it around and going about the streets and the local pitch every spare minute I had, pretending to be Marco van Basten. The Dutch striker was my hero, and I would love to have played in the magnificent AC Milan side that he helped to so many successes. In footballing terms, it was a tragedy that he had to quit playing because of a knee injury when he still had at least three or four years at the top left in him. He is now head coach of the Netherlands, and he's already proved a success in the short space of time that he has been in charge.

The first time I can remember being involved in an organised game of football was when I was 11 years old. My father, who helped coach the Montana Under-18 and Under-21 sides, took me along to the stadium for a game. I was four or five years younger than the rest and a good bit smaller, but I wasn't shy about asking for the ball. In fact, I think they were all fed up listening to my squeaky little voice demanding a pass all the time. The older boys used to ignore me because they presumed I wasn't up to much, but once I battled for possession and showed them what I could do, they started to take notice.

My father was great in respect to my ambition to become a professional footballer. He always encouraged me to put football before school, and sometimes I would miss my lessons to practise and improve my game. My dad knew this but didn't mind. As long as I had a ball at my feet, he accepted me ducking out of the odd class here and there. I think, at times, the school also knew what was going on but never interfered.

My progression in the game was good, and my desire to become a footballer intensified as I grew up. The first time I thought it might happen for real was when I played my first few games for Montana as a teenager. I worked my way up through their youth sides and made my debut for the first team when I was still in school; I was only 16 years old. It was 1996, and I was sitting in a maths class. Suddenly, there was a knock on the door and the Montana coach Boyan Gergov was there with a release paper signed by the headmaster for my teacher. It allowed me to leave the class and play for Montana in a cup tie. The headmaster was happy letting me go because he was a fan of the team and wanted me to help them win an important match against Levski Sofia, the strongest side in Bulgaria at the time. The night before, I'd scored two goals against Botev in an Under-21 game and played really well. Gergov was at the game and obviously felt I was capable of doing a decent job for the first team.

We drew 1–1 in the cup tie. I played the last 20 minutes and really enjoyed it. I was made to feel welcome by everyone. Even the boys in the first team seemed to be glad to see me as they knew I had a decent chance of going on to become a good player. Many of my classmates came to watch the game after school, and they were really proud of me. I felt elated the next day going into school, but I wasn't signing autographs or anything like that. They don't go in for that kind of thing so much in Bulgaria.

There wasn't a hint of jealousy from anyone that I'd made my Montana debut. My classmates accepted that I wanted to play football and were happy for me that I was getting closer to achieving my goal. It was just the way I would have felt for the ones that wanted to become a car mechanic, a doctor, a schoolteacher or a dancer. We all encouraged each other to do everything possible to make our dreams turn into reality.

My next match was a week later against Litex Lovech. They needed a point from the game to avoid relegation. There were about ten minutes to go and the score was 2–2 when Gergov decided it was time for me to go on. He told me to defend and make sure that we didn't lose the game. I played on the left-hand side of midfield and ended up scoring the winner with a left-foot shot from about 20 yards. I was delighted but noticed a couple of the older players in the Montana team didn't appear to be very happy with me. I couldn't understand why, but it was later pointed out to me that they were probably counting on a bung of some kind or another if Lovech got the point they needed to avoid relegation.

The bonus that we received for our win was around £40 so with my first wage I took my Montana teammates out to celebrate. Mind you, I'm not sure if all of them came out with me that night!

The other pleasing thing for me that day was that Grisha

Ganchev, the president of Lovech, wanted to sign me straight away, but it wasn't possible because staying put was the best thing for me to do at that time. He then offered Montana money to make sure that his team had first option to buy me when the time came for me to be sold. However, Lovech had no chance of getting me when CSKA came calling the next season. Ganchev was livid that I'd joined CSKA, and every time I see him, even to this day, he reminds me about that goal and the fact he didn't get the chance to sign me.

In many ways, it would have been easier for me to sign for his side as joining CSKA could have become complicated. You see, I grew up as a Levski Sofia fan but signed for CSKA. It wasn't a problem for me, but some of the fans had an issue with it. I suppose it would be like me being a big Celtic fan and signing for Rangers. Sometimes I'd get a bit of stick from the supporters, but it was never anything serious. I grew to love CSKA, and I never had any problem giving 100 per cent for them.

My father and mother were so proud of me. They had sporting backgrounds and were glad to see me take the same route. My dad used to be a footballer and also coached the Montana Under-18 and Under-21 sides. My mother represented Bulgaria at long-distance running and high jumping but stopped to look after me and my brother. She still takes care of herself now and likes to go running every day to keep in good shape.

Playing for CSKA was a big step up from Montana. I came from a small town, and this was a move to the big city; I was, understandably, nervous. At CSKA I shared a flat with Martin Petrov. We had fun together, and it was good that I was only about an hour away from Montana. It meant my parents were close, and I could go home if we had a couple of days off.

I still had to continue my studies while I was at CSKA. My last year of school was difficult because I had to study on my own and return to my school in Montana once every four months to sit exams. It was difficult to discipline myself to put the time and effort in, but despite playing truant in the early days, I was delighted to eventually pass exams in geography, maths, geology, economics, English – although it didn't help me when I first arrived in Glasgow – and music. I was proud to have achieved my grades after spending so many years at school. Of course, I always wanted to be a footballer. That was my priority and the thing that I channelled most of my energies into. I suppose it didn't matter whether I passed any exams or not, but it gave me personal satisfaction to succeed and gain my certificates.

5

The Army

As a teenager in Bulgaria you don't enjoy the freedom of Western kids – there's only one choice and that's to go through national service when you're 18. There are only two get-outs: if you're disabled or homosexual. Since I'm neither I had no option but to join the army in January 1998. The branch I enrolled with was called a Sport Army Camp attached to CSKA Sofia. The club formed it many years ago especially for sportsmen with futures in their chosen field, whether it was football, wrestling or volleyball. I was placed there because, at that time, every player around my age on the books of CSKA Sofia had to go.

It probably isn't as tough as the army camps you go to when you want to become a real soldier, but it was still demanding and hard going. There was no question of the guys in our camp wanting to fight for their country in a war or anything like that. The only consolation was we were able to combine our sport with our national service.

It might sound like an easy way out, but it's not as simple as claiming you're interested in sport just to avoid joining the real army! It was almost impossible to cheat the system. I know some footballers who were attached to clubs for a year or so before their national service time arrived, and they thought they'd be going to the Sport Army Camp. Then the clubs informed the government that they weren't good enough to be footballers, and they were packed off to the real army instead! National service used to last two years, but by the time I had to do it, it was only eighteen months. Now they've reduced it again to nine months.

It was a tough time for me, though, because I had just signed for CSKA Sofia, and all I wanted to do was concentrate on playing football and establish myself in the first team. But I wasn't allowed to play for CSKA in the Bulgarian league for the first few months. I had to play for the army team against other divisions around the country – including our local rivals, the Levski Sofia army team. We were fortunate enough to win the league, and I contributed by scoring 14 goals. We received a beautiful gold medal for our success. I did get games for CSKA in my second season and scored seven goals in nearly fifty games.

Once I settled down in the army camp, I have to be honest and say I didn't find it too bad. I made a lot of good friends that I still keep in touch with to this day. Mind you, the first day I joined I was put in a dormitory with five other guys – and four of us had the surname Petrov! When the name Petrov was shouted, the four of us all answered, 'Yes, sir.'

The Petrov in the bed next to me was a wrestler, and it turned out that a few months earlier I had been fighting in the street with him over a girl. I think his girlfriend fancied me, and he wasn't happy at her giving me some attention. He confronted me, and the next thing I knew we were rolling about on the deck of a pavement café. I managed to hold my own, which was good considering the size and strength of the guy, whose first name I can't remember.

The fight lasted a few minutes, and we then both went our separate ways. I had no idea I'd been fighting with a sportsman, never mind a wrestler, and he didn't know anything about me. We didn't talk for the first week, but then we got on fine together. I don't think he's with the same girl any more!

My spell in the army started when I was sent the papers to sign up. Then, on 3 January 1998, I moved to the barracks in Sofia – about ten minutes' drive from CSKA's stadium – on a full-time basis. It was a complete shock to the system. The size of the camp was about the same as eight football pitches. The facilities were basic, but they included a small gym and a football pitch, so we didn't complain. In saying that, if we had complained it wouldn't have made any difference.

Being away from home in a barracks surrounded by a group of men took a while to get used to. As soon as I was assigned a bed and had picked up my uniform, I had to shave my hair off! OK, it's the army, but I really like my hair – most people in Bulgaria have a thing about it, actually – so I wasn't too happy. It was a number one cut right into the scalp, but I got used to it in the end, I suppose. It became a weekly event, and I actually ended up cutting it myself.

Apart from that, I was told in the letter before I arrived that I had to bring other basics with me like toilet paper, a brush, toothpaste and toothbrush, polish, and a needle and thread. We weren't allowed to personalise our dorms by putting up posters or displaying family photographs.

One of the first things we were told to do was sew our badges and numbers onto our shirts and jackets. That was a problem – I didn't know one end of a needle from the other. I was so bad that Martin Petrov, who plays beside me in the national team, had to do it for me. He was one of my room-mates in the Sport Army Camp, along with a few wrestlers, and, if nothing else, we all had a laugh together.

One night there was an almighty fight in our dormitory when the six of us played a game of cards. One of the boxers accused one of the wrestlers of cheating, and it all kicked off. They were getting stuck into each other. Punches and kicks were flying everywhere, but, eventually, the boxer got the better of his wrestling 'friend'.

Seeing that fracas put me off playing cards with them again. I would never cheat but thought that even if I made an innocent mistake during a game, it might cost me my front teeth.

A lot of stories were passed around at night to keep our spirits up, and although some of the guys were quite crazy they were well worth listening to. They used to get up during the night to practise lifting up their beds and would challenge each other to arm wrestling contests. One day, one of them lifted up a chair and it broke, so he was ordered by the officers in charge to do extra cleaning duties.

Unfortunately, the first two weeks that I was in camp I took ill. It was nothing serious but enough to keep me in bed and limit what I could do. However, it meant that I missed the shooting lessons and didn't get a chance to practise with a rifle. The first time I held one was in the exam with the rest of the boys.

It felt *really* strange to hold a loaded gun. For starters, it was heavy. I had never held a real one before, and, to be honest, I was terrified. Anyone standing anywhere near me should have been too! The exam consisted of firing five bullets at a target one hundred metres away and then another five at a target two hundred metres away. My football shooting may be good, but my rifle shooting was really poor. In fact, I was an embarrassment! I didn't hit the targets once – didn't even graze them. What made it worse was that I was the only one to fail the test. Thank God I never had to go to war for my country. With me on the front line our enemy would have been completely safe! That wasn't even the end of it. I had to declare when my gun was empty and take the target back, but I totally forgot. Thankfully, they didn't realise either. I was lucky because I would have ended up with black marks against my name and that resulted in a fine. It would maybe have been about a pound. That may not seem like a lot to people in the West, but you have to remember that our wages at the time were only about five or six pounds a *month*.

After the first month at camp, we had a special day to mark our arrival. It was a big ceremony in the CSKA stadium in which we had to march in front of a crowd with the national flag. Part of the ceremony was a public declaration that we were now soldiers and would do anything to defend our country.

It may not have been ideal in the camp, but the one good thing about it was that it meant I was allowed to get on with my football career and could start training properly with the team again. All the other guys, like the volleyball players and athletes, could do the same. It was a big relief to us all.

Even though we were in a special unit, we still found it difficult to get the army's full trust. They sent a special armed car to take me and Martin Petrov to training every day and bring us back again. Apparently, the reason we were always under constant watch was because some of the guys had tried to run away in the past, and they didn't want it to happen again. I don't know about the other boys, but I wouldn't have considered even for one second doing a runner. You'd have to be mad. Why would I want to go on the run for the rest of my life? The authorities would always track you down. And the punishment? Well, I don't know exactly what they would have done, but it's fair to guess that it wouldn't have been very pleasant.

Some people might have found it tough going, but I didn't find the whole experience too taxing. On a typical day, you'd get up just before six in the morning, have a wash and a shave, iron a clean shirt and get yourself dressed. The worst thing you could do was try to sneak an extra five minutes in bed and end up rushing about. One morning, one of the guys was up against the clock and couldn't find his razor. He ended up shaving himself with a knife and cut his face to shreds! His face was in such a state that he required medical attention, and he was relieved of his duties for the rest of the day. With blood streaming from his neck and cheeks I'm sure he wished he'd got out of bed ten minutes earlier that day!

After getting ready, we had to make sure that our bed was made properly for the inspection from the commanders and that our little bit of the room was tidy. I had three or four drawers and a couple of shelves for my belongings so it wasn't exactly a hardship to keep it clean. We would then stand for the national anthem and go for breakfast. Most days it would be toast and honey, although on occasion we wouldn't get any breakfast if someone had stepped out of line. If one of us broke a rule – like talking during the meal – then everyone suffered, and we would all be thrown out of the breakfast room to get on with the rest of the day on an empty stomach. It happened a couple of times. Think of the guilt you would feel when you've got a room full of hungry, angry soldiers to answer to. Thankfully, I was never guilty of depriving any of us of our breakfast.

After a roll-call, we would go for our lessons. These lasted about two or three hours and were mostly about army regulations, such as who's who in the chain of command and what to do if the emergency bell went off. Then we'd get a bit of exercise, maybe running and stretching, and after that we would have some basic cleaning duties to do.

At other times, we would learn how to march properly, using the correct steps at the right times. Normally, that lesson would last about an hour, but I remember one day it took us over *five hours* because one of the soldiers couldn't get the routine right.

That was nothing compared with the last ten days of our first month, though, when we had to perfect a routine for our first public parade. Three hours' practice in the morning and then four more hours in the afternoon: seven hours a day of that stuff was more torture than I could imagine.

Then again, even *that* wasn't as bad as one of our shooting practices. Everyone from my house went out to shoot in the snow with ten bullets each. No problem, you would think, except that, afterwards, we had to collect the empty cartridges and hand them back to the officer in charge. Most of the guys found their ten, but four were missing, and we weren't allowed to go home until *every* one was accounted for. It took us four and a half hours to find the rest of them. We had to get down on our hands and knees to dig deep into the snow, and it was dark when we eventually got back to the base.

That day was probably the coldest and most frustrated I have ever felt in my life, but it taught me a valuable lesson about teamwork. Even though I located my spent shells, I had to help the other soldiers find theirs. It meant we all put in the same effort – nobody benefited from doing their own thing.

Lunch was usually quite early, at about 10 o'clock in the morning, and maybe consisted of some nice meat or salad. However, we weren't allowed to eat until the captain was ready. Sometimes we'd be forced to wait outside the dining room until he was ready to sit down. That was really hard to take because I have a big appetite and spent most of my 18 months there desperate for my next meal. There just wasn't enough food to satisfy me, and I lost weight in the first month. It wasn't a huge amount, just a few pounds. After our first month we were allowed visitors, so my parents and friends would bring me in a little parcel of extra food and chocolate to keep me going.

Those first four weeks were pretty tough because we weren't allowed outside the barracks or allowed any visitors. The only line of communication with the outside world was with an occasional phone call or letter. After that, I was allowed to leave for a couple of hours a day to train with CSKA Sofia but had to come back straight away once I had finished. I sometimes managed to persuade the driver to stop at a shop so that I could buy some sweets and things to give us something extra to look forward to at the end of the day. The volleyball players weren't so lucky. They had to do all their training inside the camp!

Our main meal of the day was at seven o'clock, and what a relief it was. It was always decent, too. We had different things most days: meat, potatoes and nice salads. We then had some spare time after our dinner to relax and play board or card games or whatever. At 9.30 p.m., we all assembled in the main hall to sing the national anthem again, and then it was to bed with all lights out by 10 p.m.

The guys in our room also had a rota of other duties to carry out, which changed every two days. Sometimes you would have to guard the room all day to make sure nobody from another dorm broke in to mess up your barracks and get you punished. At other times, you would have to sleep on the floor to get used to not having a mattress. Maybe we'd have to patrol the grounds outside to make sure no intruders got in. That was a tough shift: carrying a fully loaded rifle all night, concentrating really hard and desperately trying not to fall asleep.

One time, one of the soldiers who was up in the post house during the night didn't notice someone coming into the barracks and letting off fireworks! He ended up with 20 days in solitary confinement as a punishment. Thankfully, nothing like that happened to me. The only time I remember being punished was after we had a game of football in our room against the officers when we were supposed to be sleeping. The captain caught us, and I was ordered to clean the five flights of stairs in the barracks for four hours a day, for four days. That was a nightmare, and it was during times like that the temptation to chuck it all in welled up inside me. I'd be on my hands and knees scrubbing away with the brush, and just when I thought they looked spotless and fit enough to pass inspection, I would see the captain pass me by on his way up to the top of the stairs with a bucket of soapy water. He would pour it downstairs from the top, and I would have to start again. It sounds cruel but that's the army for you. My arms and thighs ached for about a fortnight afterwards – I felt like Popeye. The biggest crime in the camp, though, was getting caught with alcohol. When one of the rooms in another house got caught with a large stash of booze they were all put in solitary for one month.

I finally signed out early in the summer of 1999. On my last day, I had to sign all the release papers and hand back the uniforms. For some reason I had lost one of my spare uniforms and ended up having to pay for it. It cost about £20, which is a lot of money in Bulgaria considering the average monthly wage is so low.

When my passing-out day finally came it was a proud moment for me and the rest of the guys. My parents were there for the ceremony, but it won't be a day we'll remember too fondly after I nearly killed another soldier by accident! As part of our passing-out ceremony, we had to perform a drill involving the rifle, which we had been practising in the weeks leading up to the event. They called out my name, and I had to do a little routine with the gun, spinning it about a couple of times. Stupidly, I didn't realise there was a bayonet on the end of it, and I nearly cut off the head of the soldier standing in line behind me! Fortunately, he just saw it coming and managed to pull his head out of the way in time. The commanders weren't too happy as they wanted it all to be perfect, but we managed to have a laugh about it all in the end.

There was a party on the final night. I hadn't planned to go to it because I had a cup tie for CSKA Sofia the next day, but at 11 o'clock the guys talked me into going out to a disco. I was persuaded to go because we had spent a year and a half of our lives in each other's pockets but might not see one another again. I stayed up with them until 6.30 a.m., although I didn't drink any alcohol. I only got about two hours' sleep, but it worked out well for me because we won 1–0, and I scored the goal from a free-kick.

There were elements of life in the army that I did enjoy. I made good friends and still keep in touch with the wrestler Peter Ivanov, who is now a personal bodyguard. He gets plenty of work in Bulgaria! I also played for the army football team, and we won the league that included Bulgaria's four other army sides. I scored 13 goals and still treasure my winner's medal. At least that kept the commander of my base happy – it had been a few years since his team had won the league, and he also had a big rivalry with a commander from another camp. It must have meant a lot to him – and we were given ten days off for winning!

Despite the many happy memories I have, it wasn't all plain sailing. Some of the high-ranking officers were very tough, and there was just no pleasing them. However, one of them had a real soft spot for me because he was a huge CSKA Sofia fan and was desperate to find out all the gossip. He would invite me into his office for a cup of tea and a chat, although some of the other soldiers weren't too pleased about that. One of the lads tried to wind him up one day by wearing a Levski Sofia T-shirt. His sense of humour didn't stretch that far. The officer ripped the shirt off the soldier's back and set fire to it in the bin right in front of him!

All in all, though, I think the army was a good thing and a rewarding experience at that stage of my life. It taught me discipline and respect, and I have tried to apply those principles to all elements of my life since.

6

My Celtic Managers

A pivotal moment in my Celtic career was the night we lost 3–1 to Inverness Caley Thistle in the Tennent's Scottish Cup in February 2000. It was an embarrassing result, and there was absolutely no excuse for it. I wasn't available for selection that night as I was in Chile with the Bulgarian national team. I had an arrangement with Mark Burchill whereby I would call him just after the game finished to find out the result.

We had lost 3–2 to Hearts in a league game at Parkhead the previous Saturday after being two goals ahead. The boys' heads were down after that result. More than 50,000 of our fans had let us know exactly how they felt about the loss to the Tynecastle side, and the boys knew it was important to get back into the winning habit against Inverness. The pressure was on, but we believed a game against a First Division side would give us the ideal chance to get back on track. How wrong we were. I thought we would win three or four nil, and when I checked the result on my hotel-room TV I was sure that there had been a misprint: 'Celtic – 1, Inverness Caledonian Thistle – 3'. It had to be wrong.

You Can Call Me Stan

I phoned about an hour after the final whistle and was shocked when Burchie confirmed the result. My English wasn't particularly good at the time, and I said to him, 'What was the score?'

'We lost 3–1,' he replied. 'Stan, it's absolute bedlam. The fans are going crazy. I'm still in the dressing-room and can't say too much just now. It's not a good time to talk. Phone me back in a wee while, and I'll be able to tell you everything.' I couldn't believe what I was hearing as Burchie also told me some of the things that had happened at half-time between Mark Viduka, Eric Black and John Barnes.

While they were still locked in the dressing-room, Burchie and the rest of the boys were hoping that the anger and bad atmosphere would eventually disappear. The Celtic fans were furious and around 500 had gathered outside the main entrance to demonstrate, most of them calling for Barnes's head. I phoned Burchie again about 20 minutes later, and he was still in the dressing-room. He told me the atmosphere outside the ground was frightening and that there were bound to be major repercussions. I'm so glad I wasn't there for the post-match trouble. Most of the players had to be escorted by a security guard through the angry crowd to get to their cars. The players took all sorts of abuse, and it must have been a tough night for everyone connected with the club – fans, players and staff.

Of course, something major did happen, and Barnes ended up the biggest loser when he lost his job the next day. I never got the chance to say goodbye to him and have never met him since that fateful day, although I have watched him on Five presenting his football show. His assistant Eric Black and coach Terry McDermott were also sacked. I was still in Chile when all this happened, but it made the news in South America, and, of course, I was phoning Burchie and my other friends in Glasgow to keep up to date with events as they unfolded.

Part of me felt sorry for Barnes as I believed he was a good coach. Maybe if he has a bit of good fortune he could do well in management at another club. I'll never forget that he was the man who signed me, and I still believe that he had the best interests of the club and the dressing-room at heart, but, for whatever reason, it just didn't work out for him at Celtic. One of the reasons may have been that he struggled to motivate the dressing-room at crucial times. It could also be argued that Barnes's lack of success had a lot to do with the fact that he was without Henrik Larsson for four months of the season, after the Swede broke his leg against Lyon in a UEFA Cup tie. Any team and any manager would have found it difficult to win without their main goal scorer.

When we lost Henrik, Barnes moved quickly to tie up Ian Wright as his short-term replacement. Ian had been a magnificent goal scorer throughout his career, and his exploits have ensured his place as an Arsenal legend. He was a bright and bubbly character who seemed to have a constant smile on his face and his laugh was infectious. He is without doubt the happiest man I've ever met in football.

Wrighty loved playing jokes on the boys. The one I remember most is when we were away to either Hibs or Hearts, and he was on the bench. He thought it would be funny to hide the physio's medical bag down the side of the technical area, and when Brian Scott came to use it, he started to panic because his bag was nowhere to be seen. As Scottie searched frantically around the dugout, Wrighty was sitting behind him laughing his head off like a naughty schoolboy!

A few of the players were truly relieved and delighted when Barnes was forced to go. I didn't feel as strongly as that, but I was pleased in a way because part of me felt that it could signal a turning point for me at Celtic. Under a new manager I could show the club exactly what I was capable of and finally reward them for putting faith in me. To achieve that, however, I knew I had to play in my best position, which was in central midfield. John Barnes had played me at right-back and left midfield, and I prayed that the new man – whoever that was going to be – would start me in my best position.

Playing out of position meant I wasn't doing myself justice at

Celtic, but my international career was also suffering as a result. It got so bad during that period that, at one point, I was warned by a member of Bulgaria's coaching staff that I had to get my Celtic career back on track or my international prospects would suffer. I took that warning on board and knew I had to turn things around under the new manager.

Kenny Dalglish was appointed as team boss, coming 'downstairs' from his role as Director of Football to inherit a job that was fraught with pitfalls. I returned from Chile on the Friday and when I got back to Parkhead I immediately sensed a strange atmosphere around the place. There was also an obvious lack of confidence and a real flatness, which was entirely understandable after the disastrous result against Inverness and the fallout in the days after it. Dalglish tried his best to improve morale and held one-to-one sessions with a few of the players to try to lift spirits. He wanted to get as many of us as possible onside with him.

I took to him straight away and had a feeling things were going to work out between us. I remember he took me aside shortly after his appointment, and I immediately got a good feeling about working with him in the weeks and months ahead. He spoke to me on my own and said, 'Stiliyan, it's not been easy for you, but I have every confidence it will work out well for you at Celtic. You are going to be a big part of my plans. I want you to impose yourself on a game and not be afraid to express yourself. Be more confident, don't be afraid.' Interestingly, Dalglish felt I had been happy to go through a game without making the contribution I was capable of but knew it was down to a lack of confidence, rather than me not being bothered about playing for the jersey.

His first game in charge was away to Dundee, and it was vital that we blew away the cobwebs of the Inverness debacle by getting off to a good start under the new manager. We won 2–0, and a huge weight lifted from our shoulders.

There was still plenty of hard work ahead, but even after a couple of games under Kenny Dalglish, I was beginning to enjoy my football again. Probably for the first time since I had joined the club, I felt good about myself and was more satisfied with my game. Kenny took me aside to offer encouragement and told me I had been doing well. He also said that it was vital that I continued to show the same level of progress. It felt great that the manager had positive things to say to me.

I remember when I was still a teenager, one of my old coaches in Bulgaria told me that an average player has two or three good games in a row. A good player has four or five. A really good player has six or seven. And an excellent player has nine or ten good games in a row. I stored away those words and always strived to reach the excellent category from that day onwards. In my early days at Celtic, I wasn't even good enough for the average category, but after Kenny Dalglish spoke to me, I thought I had a chance of finally reaching the highest point. He also told me to try and forget about my early form and to only concentrate on the future.

At that time, I would have been happy if Kenny had been given the job on a permanent basis because I respected him and responded to his methods. I don't know if he was offered the position permanently, although I suspect at some stage during his three-month reign he must have been.

Kenny also brought in Tommy Burns to help him during his short tenure as he was short of numbers after the departure of Barnes, Black and McDermott. I like Tommy – he is a very good person. Gordon Strachan has appointed him as a member of his backroom team, and I'm pleased to see him back with the first-team squad.

Kenny and Tommy changed the training routines, and there seemed to be a happier atmosphere at the club. The players were responding well to the new regime. We were laughing and joking and enjoying going into work in the morning. I was also learning every day, and because I was enjoying my football again, I started to go back to training in the afternoons. A definite change for the better.

The happier times continued into March of that season when we managed to win a trophy, beating Aberdeen 2–0 in the final of the

CIS Cup at Hampden. It was important to get some silverware to stop Rangers from doing back-to-back Trebles under Dick Advocaat, and we were delighted finally to give the fans something to cheer about after what had been a difficult season. We celebrated that night by going to a lovely Chinese restaurant in Glasgow, and we really enjoyed ourselves. It was such a relief to win something after the season we had been through. I gave my CIS Cup medal to Brian Wilson because he deserved it for all he had done for me. Without his help and support, I wouldn't have been there to pick it up.

After our Hampden win the feeling that Kenny might be appointed permanently increased, but when it became public knowledge that he wasn't up for it, the club started to look elsewhere. Guus Hiddink appeared to be favourite to get the manager's job, and the dressing-room seemed to be satisfied with that. He had a good track record at both club and international level, and that experience would be invaluable in helping us to stop Rangers. The thought of two Dutchmen going head to head on either side of the Old Firm also added extra spice to the whole scenario.

Although everyone inside Celtic Park had been telling me that Hiddink's appointment was rubber-stamped, by the time I left Glasgow for my summer holidays in Bulgaria the club still didn't have a new boss. I was continually on the phone to Brian and Burchie to find out what was happening, as I was desperate to know who our new gaffer would be. You expect a new manager to be given money to spend on players and wonder if he'll use that transfer cash to buy someone who plays in your position.

Despite the promises, the arrival of Hiddink never materialised, and, eventually, Martin O'Neill was appointed as the new manager in the summer of 2000. Forget about star players arriving, securing Martin O'Neill must go down as one of the best signings the club has ever made. Not since Jock Stein was appointed has a manager had such an impact at Celtic. I didn't really know anything about him, but I quickly learned that he was a passionate Celtic fan from

Northern Ireland, who had enjoyed a successful playing career and had won a couple of cups as manager of Leicester City. My investigations also made me realise that he had never failed at any club that he had ever been at, and I knew he would do whatever was necessary to make Celtic the top team in Scotland again.

From my point of view, I'm so glad that he was appointed, as I really don't know where I would be now without him. Although, initially, it was Kenny Dalglish that helped me to regain my form and confidence, I truly believe that it was Martin O'Neill that saved my career. Back in Bulgaria, I sat for long periods during the summer of 2000 questioning what I wanted to achieve as a footballer and pondering my future with Celtic. I told myself that I had to work harder than ever to impress the new manager and show everyone in Scotland how good a player I could be.

I had a chat with Martin O'Neill during that year's pre-season tour in Ireland and Denmark to find out what he thought of me and if I had a future at Celtic with him as manager. He was straight to the point and asked me what position I preferred to play in. When I told him it was the centre of midfield he promised me a chance to play there so he could see what I was like. By giving me that opportunity, there could be no excuses if things didn't work out for me during his stewardship of the team.

He also told me to improve my fitness if I wanted to play in his team. I understood his concerns because my fitness had deteriorated during the summer. In fact, I had put on around a stone in weight, which was both frightening and embarrassing. I'm the type of person that has to work nearly every day to maintain my shape. If I'm eating a lot and having a few drinks during the holidays while not exercising then the weight piles on. I worked hard to lose those extra pounds when O'Neill arrived, and I thank our fitness coach Jim Hendry for all his help in sorting me out.

I think it's safe to say that Martin O'Neill obviously rated me as a player in those first few weeks, and I was really happy when he gave me a new contract after he had been at the club for just three or four months. I was pleased to get that bit extra every month in my wage packet. It made a difference, and, to be honest, I thought I deserved it. He subsequently gave me another new deal and wage rise, and, again, it was good of him to sort that out, but I felt that I deserved that contract as well. I'm now tied to the club until the summer of 2007, and I'm happy playing for Celtic under the type of manager I want to play for. However, now that Martin has left the club, I wish him well for the future.

Overall, I thought O'Neill was a very clever and talented man. He ensured we had a great atmosphere in the dressing-room, and, along with his backroom staff of John Robertson and Steve Walford, he really helped build team spirit. They treated us all like adults; small things like being allowed to play the music that we wanted in the dressing-room before games helped.

Also, every Friday we played a game between the young players and the old guys in the squad, and the worst player had to wear the dreaded yellow jersey. The management had introduced the idea at Leicester and brought it with them to help keep the atmosphere light and the players happy – apart from the guy who wears the yellow jersey, of course!

It's not just the management who help make our dressing-room a happy place. The players play their part too. Chris Sutton is a great guy to have around. He is a fun-loving bloke, but you have to keep an eye on him. He has been known to throw his teammates' clothes in the shower, and on the day it was our PR man Iain Jamieson's birthday, Sutty grabbed him and threw him into the bath with all his clothes on. Iain was soaked and had to borrow a tracksuit from John Clark's kit room to wear for the rest of the day.

Jackie McNamara is also someone who makes me laugh. He does a great take-off of some of the *Chewin' The Fat* characters that used to have the boys in stitches. Jackie was our team captain and a tremendous servant to the club. I was so pleased to be at the Hilton Hotel in Glasgow in May 2004 when he won the Scottish Football Writers' Player of the Year award. It was well deserved. He also had a great testimonial season after serving the football club for so long.

However, Jackie is no longer with us at Celtic, and I still find that hard to take. He has been a big loss, and Wolves are lucky to have him. I spoke to him on the day he signed for Glenn Hoddle's club, and he was quite upset at having to leave. I was upset for him. He has been a sad loss and was the last guy I expected to leave us. It was a parting of the ways that should never have happened.

After we beat Dundee United 1–0 in the 2005 Tennent's Scottish Cup final, I sat with Jackie in the bath and felt rotten that I wasn't going to be able to play in his testimonial match the next day against the Republic of Ireland. I was ordered back to Bulgaria to prepare for a game against Croatia and had no choice but to leave straight away for Glasgow Airport after the match. I desperately wanted to play in his game, to honour my friend and team up again with Lubo Moravcik and Henrik Larsson. Jackie understood my situation.

Despite not playing in the testimonial, he still gave me the computer that was a gift to every player that took part in his benefit match. The computer has a screensaver of his smiling face on it, so I'll never be able to forget him. Jackie's cheeky grin cheapens the look of the computer, but I'll forgive him for that!

John Hartson is another of my teammates that I find very warm and generous. He loves the company of the boys in the dressing-room, and you always find him the same every day – happy and up for a game of football.

Stan Varga is another good friend of mine. We come from similar parts of the world and have a bit in common. He has been a great signing for Celtic, and his family have been a good addition off the park as we are all close and often go out for dinner together.

Juninho is another great person, and I'm sorry things didn't work out for him at Celtic. I spent a lot of time with him at the stadium and socially, and he was desperate to be a success at Celtic. He also liked to have a bit of fun at the ground.

Despite the jokes, none of the players takes the carry-on too far and we all know the boundaries. We are also aware that a manager knows everything that is going on at a club and makes sure it's run the way he wants it. For example, Martin fined me a couple of times for poor timekeeping. The most worrying incident was when I was late for the coach leaving Parkhead to go to our hotel for our first ever Champions League game. It was a Tuesday night and we were playing against Rosenborg the following evening. I was ten minutes late, and I think the gaffer fined me £1,000. I deserved it. Of course, that day was 11 September 2001, and the game was cancelled because of the terrorist atrocities in America. The gaffer never forgot who he had fined and would remind the guys if they hadn't paid up their dues.

On the football front, his team-talks were exceptional, and the way he motivated players was unbelievable. He didn't talk for hours on end, he just kept it short and sharp and said what he had to. That's the way he was before a game and even more so at half-time when there's only a few minutes to say the important stuff.

I remember his first ever half-time team-talk as Celtic manager in a pre-season match in Ireland. We weren't playing particularly well – as is often the case for a lot of clubs in pre-season games – and I think a few of the players thought the gaffer wouldn't be too bothered. Well, without leaving anyone in any doubt about his feelings, he told a couple of players that they hadn't played to the standard he expected of someone in his football team and that if they didn't improve on quality and commitment they wouldn't get a game. From that moment on, every player knew the score with the manager – you either gave it everything you had or you would be looking for another club. From that first day, he set the standards that he expected, and I'm just glad I managed to live up to them and hope that I can maintain those standards for the new manager.

The manager is on record as saying that the half-time team-talk is one of the most important times of the week. And I think if you look at the amount of games in which we were behind or drawing at half-time and then went on to win, it gives an indication of what a difference they can make.

Martin O'Neill would criticise you if he felt you hadn't played well, but he would do it behind closed doors and not in public. He didn't criticise for the sake of it – there was always merit in his judgement – he just hated losing football games. I'm glad to say we didn't lose too often under him, and hopefully that trend will continue under Gordon Strachan.

In saying that, one night O'Neill did have a go at me. It was after we lost 3–2 at home to Aberdeen in the early part of the 2004–05 season. We were 2–0 down, came back to level the game, then Aberdeen scored a late winner.

O'Neill was furious after the game and blamed me for one or two things. I didn't think I deserved to be criticised and told him so in front of the rest of the lads in the dressing-room. I was really sharp with him. It was totally out of character for me because I'm normally very placid, and if I'm taking a verbal kicking I usually stay quiet and accept it. He wasn't happy. I was called into the gaffer's office the next day, and we spoke about a few things. I apologised for answering back, and he admitted he wasn't entirely blameless in the whole situation, which was honest of him. O'Neill was always honest. From day one he told every player they would get a chance, and if it didn't work out, they would go their separate ways with no hard feelings.

There is a popular saying in football that no individual is bigger than the club, but Martin O'Neill was probably as near as you'll get to that logic being dismissed. He is a top-class manager and, in John Robertson and Steve Walford, has two top-class men beside him. Martin's importance to Celtic and the positives that he brought to the club between 2000 and 2005 cannot be underestimated. He put Celtic back on the map by winning three SPL championships and re-established respect for the club on the European scene. He will be in the thoughts of many chairmen throughout Europe. He has been one of the most successful managers in Britain over the past seven or eight years and that attracts attention.

O'Neill is also the kind of guy that makes you want to become a manager, but I'm not really sure if I am cut out to be one. There's a lot to think about before I'll ever get round to making that decision and maybe in around ten years I will have changed my mind. I have been involved in coaching kids over here, and I enjoy that side of the game. I help train the Celtic Boys Club, and it is great to see the kids enjoy working with a first-team player who has taken the time to visit them. I also help in my friend's coaching school, which is good fun. It brings me enormous satisfaction to see a kid learning to do keepy-uppy or strike the ball sweetly with either foot.

I don't know for sure what I will do when I finish playing, but, at this stage, I want to stay in the game at some level. Maybe coaching kids will be my thing. Children simply love playing football, and they don't moan or get too down if they lose a game. First and foremost it's all about fun for them, and when you're enjoying yourself you're also learning more. Kids are not greedy for money or looking to move to another club, they just want to play for the love of the game. Obviously, many do hope that it leads to them becoming good enough to make a career in the game, just like I did when I was a kid.

Being a youth coach has no real pressure. It's all about teaching the kids good habits and letting them express themselves. On the other hand, I don't believe there is much enjoyment in top-level management. A lot of managers at big clubs look stressed out and miserable, and I don't see the fun in being under that kind of constant pressure. If things aren't going well, the buck stops with the manager. Worryingly, and wrongly, it can start to affect your family. You don't want your kids to be taunted at school or your wife to be verbally abused at the supermarket because of football results. Sure, managers are well paid for the pressure that they have to endure, but why would I want to get involved in a career that saw me get out of bed every day worrying whether I am going to lose a game and then my job? No thanks. That would definitely put me in an early grave.

I don't have any sporting hobbies away from football, and I should perhaps learn to play golf to give me some form of relaxation. I hear it is good to spend three or four hours on the golf course, so that might be just the thing I turn to when I stop playing. Yes, I can picture myself getting a nice tan as I tour around the beautiful courses in Spain and Portugal, playing a round with a few friends. That scenario sounds much better – and healthier – than coming close to a heart attack in the dugout.

I know many pros have said the same as me at this stage of their career and ended up getting sucked into management, but I'd like to think I won't be tempted down that road when I decide to hang up my boots. However, if the chance to manage Celtic ever came along, well, that might just be a different story.

The Celtic job was too good an opportunity for Gordon Strachan to resist when he was offered the chance to replace Martin in May 2005. I knew quite a bit about him from his time in England as a manager and media pundit, but I wanted more knowledge about him when he was appointed and so asked around a few people for further information. The feedback I received was all positive.

Gordon had been out of the game for about 15 months when he accepted the Celtic job. Prior to that he had been manager of Southampton, but he quit because he needed a hip operation and wanted to travel the world with his wife. He used his extended holiday period for pleasure but also to pick up tips from a variety of sports around the world that he could put to use in his next job.

He had apparently rejected a few job offers during his 'time-out', but the chance to take charge of Celtic is one few could ignore. The fact that he had no hesitation following in the footsteps of Martin speaks volumes for Gordon. I think lesser men wouldn't have fancied being Martin's direct replacement. However, I think that it is unfair on Martin and Gordon to make comparisons between the two: they are their own men. I'm sure, though, that Gordon would love to repeat the success Martin enjoyed during his five years at Celtic.

Gordon has already stamped his authority on the place and has made a good impression on the players. I can only speak for myself, but I think he has managed to put the difficult start he had behind him. It couldn't have been easy for him when we lost 5–0 to

Artmedia Bratislava in the Champions League qualifier. We couldn't turn the scoreline around in the next leg and we crashed out of the competition. We shouldn't have lost to them. In between the two legs, we also drew our opening league game of the season 4–4 at Motherwell. At that time, some people called for him to be sacked. That was ludicrous: completely unfair on the manager and his family. I think any manager, providing he is not having a total nightmare, deserves at least 18 months to prove he is taking a club in the right direction.

In his early days at Celtic, Gordon must have wondered what the hell was going on, but he has refused to crack and kept his composure. He has stuck to his beliefs and has put in endless hours on the training pitch with the players to try to improve them and bring them round to his way of thinking. The young players have really responded to him and they will continue to progress. The more experienced players know he is behind us and relying on us, which is the way it should be.

Being out of Europe, we have to make sure that we win the SPL championship in the 2005–06 season. All our efforts will be focused towards that goal, and there will be no excuses if we don't deliver. The manager badly wants the title, and I want to be standing there with him holding the cup aloft in May.

7

My Leg Break and
Weird Superstitions

Despite the initial problems that I faced when I joined Celtic in the summer of 1999, I have mostly happy memories of my time in Glasgow. Playing in front of the best supporters any foootballer could wish for and living in a city that has made me feel so welcome has proved better than I could ever have imagined. There is, however, one black spot in my time at Celtic, and it's without doubt the worst day of my life in football. On 14 March 2001 I broke my right leg playing in a league game against St Johnstone at McDiarmid Park.

There was nothing unusual about the events leading up to that horrific night. It was a normal day in the life of the Celtic team. We met at Parkhead, travelled to a hotel for our pre-match meal, had the team meeting and then headed to the stadium for the game. I felt really positive that night. In fact, everyone felt good as we had the CIS League Cup final to look forward to a few days later against Kilmarnock at Hampden. It was to be the first trophy we picked up on our way to winning the Treble for the first time in 32 years.

You Can Call Me Stan

I think there were about 15 minutes to go in the game against St Johnstone and we were winning 2–1 thanks to goals from Tommy Johnson and Henrik Larsson. I thought the ball was there to be won in the Saints half, and both Jim Weir of St Johnstone and I went for it. After the collision, I ended up flat out. As I lay there, I knew that there was something seriously wrong with my leg. At first, I thought my shin pad had moved out of place because I only wear small ones, but I soon knew that it was much more serious than that. I screamed out for the Celtic medical team to come on and see me. Brian Scott, our physio at that time, and the club doctor Roddy MacDonald were on the pitch in no time. They knew right away that I had broken my leg.

I was in shock. I was worried about my career, and the first thing that flashed through my mind was, 'Will I ever be able to play again?' That might sound a bit dramatic, but if you ask any footballer who has sustained a bad injury, he'll tell you that is the immediate thought that goes through your head, whether it be a leg injury, a knee injury or an ankle injury. Football is my life, my living, and the last thing I wanted was for it all to finish when I was just 21 years old. With so much to look forward to in the years to come with Celtic and Bulgaria, the prospect of having it all taken away from me would have finished me. To make matters worse – and keep my brain in overdrive – Brian and Doc Roddy offered me no guarantees that I would be able to play again.

Lying on the pitch, I wanted to curl up and die. I hoped my wife Paulina – who was my fiancée at the time – would nudge me, tell me to wake up from my nightmare and get up out of bed for training. But it wasn't a bad dream, it was real, and I was really scared. Apart from playing football, I was also getting married on 9 June later that year, and I was worried what kind of state I'd be in going down the aisle with Paulina. All these bizarre thoughts were rushing through my mind as I held my head in my hands and was stretchered off into a small room in the bowels of McDiarmid Park. Doc Roddy gave me some morphine to ease my pain and it worked. For a while.

My Leg Break and Weird Superstitions

Before I knew it, the game had finished, and the boys all came into the room to say we had won. They also told me to keep my head up, that everything was going to be fine. All the lads were really genuine, but Henrik Larsson, in particular, was very concerned. He had been through it all himself just 18 months earlier. He had suffered a horrific leg break in Lyon in a UEFA Cup tie and knew exactly how I felt. He was one of the first players to come over to me when I was on the pitch to tell me not to worry. Henrik became very important to me in my fight to regain fitness in the months ahead. Doc Roddy, Brian Scott and Jim Hendry were all also a big, big help. I couldn't have managed the four months that lay ahead without them. Ivan Nikolov, the Bulgarian national team masseur, came over to visit me for a few months and helped my recovery with a soothing massage and relaxation programme. He played a huge part in my recovery, and I'm also grateful to him for the way he helped.

From that small room in McDiarmid Park I was taken in an ambulance to a hospital in Perth, with Brian Scott and Doc Roddy accompanying me. Once we arrived, they made sure I was settled in but didn't stay the night. I was placed on a trolley bed and wheeled into a ward containing five other men who were all sleeping. An hour later, Martin O'Neill came to visit, and I was moved into my own little room. I was pleased to get some privacy as I didn't know what lay ahead in the next few hours, and the last thing I wanted was to wake up the other patients if I started to scream in pain. The boss offered words of encouragement and told me that I had had a season to be proud of. He also said that I was going to bounce back stronger than ever. Naturally, he was doing his best to cheer me up, but the only thing that was going to raise my spirits at that moment was someone guaranteeing me that I would be able to recover from the injury and play football again. Not even the gaffer could tell me that.

He stayed for about half an hour, and when he left the whole thing really started to get to me. The pain was cutting through me like a knife, and I wanted it all to end there and then. Honestly, I had never known pain like it, and I hope I never have to go through it again.

When I was 14 and 15, I broke my right arm on five different occasions in five different places while playing football, and each time I broke it I vowed never to play again. At that time, I was ready to ditch my dreams of becoming a professional footballer and thought it would be safer working as a teacher or a taxi driver – anything that didn't involve physical contact. After every break I chucked it for a couple of months to recover, but, each time, my dad talked me back into playing and assured me that injuries were part and parcel of football. He also told me that it was normal to feel depressed about being injured. I'm so glad I listened to him.

I thought a broken arm would be the nastiest thing that would ever happen to me, but the leg break was worse. Ten times worse. I desperately wanted morphine to kill the pain and begged the doctor to pump me full of it, but, first of all, I knew I had to contact Paulina and tell her what had happened. She hadn't attended the game, having decided instead to stay at home in the flat in Glasgow that we rented at that time.

I was really nervous about making the call, because I didn't want to upset Paulina or cause her to panic. As I ran through my head how I was going to break the news to her, I was praying that she hadn't heard the news on the radio or read about it on Teletext. I wanted to be the one to let her know what had happened to me. So, when I phoned I was really calm under the circumstances and asked her if she was OK. I told her that I wasn't going to be home from the football that night and that I would see her at some point the next day. Naturally, she asked me why, and I eventually told her I was lying in hospital with a broken leg. Before I had the chance to tell her that I was fine apart from the break, she was crying down the phone. She told me she was heading to Perth to spend the night with me and that I should phone our good friend Brian Wilson to ask him to drive her there.

Brian must have bombed it up the road, and was lucky not to have been stopped for speeding, because they turned up less than an hour later. I was still wearing my Celtic jersey, shorts and socks when Paulina arrived. She came over to my bed, kissed me and gave me a huge hug. It was just what I needed at that time. We had a chat with the hospital staff to find out exactly what was going to happen, and they told me that I was being transferred to Glasgow's Western Infirmary the next morning to find out the extent of the damage. I was going to be examined by Dr Billy Leitch, the man who had successfully operated on Henrik Larsson's broken leg.

I then made sure that we phoned my parents to tell them what had happened. My dad insisted that he get on a flight the next day to be with me. I was really happy that he was coming over. I had hardly put the phone down after speaking to my folks before I could feel the searing pain coursing through my leg again. I had some more morphine and can't remember much about the next few hours as I fell asleep. Brian slept in his car and Paulina slept in a chair. She has since told me that I woke up several times during the night, shouting things out and screaming, but I can't remember anything.

When I woke up at about five in the morning I knew I'd be on my way to Glasgow a few hours later for the operation. However, things didn't go as smoothly or as comfortably for me that morning as I would have liked. First of all, the ambulance didn't turn up on time. I was due to leave at 7.30 a.m. but ended up not getting away until after 9 a.m. Then, when it eventually did turn up, the driver didn't know his way to the Western Infirmary in the west end of Glasgow and had to follow Brian Wilson's car. Hardly ideal in busy traffic.

I was getting impatient and ratty and wanted more drugs to ease the pain during the journey. I couldn't believe it when the ambulance driver told me that he didn't have any and that I'd have to make do with gas and air. I was raging and let my frustrations be known, but Paulina calmed me down.

I felt more at ease when I got to the Western and looked forward to meeting Dr Leitch. I knew he would have the answers to the dozens of questions that I had for him. However, when he did arrive the only one that I remembered to ask was, 'Will I play again?' He, too, couldn't answer me for sure. He told me that he would put my leg in plaster, and, after a week, he would decide if the break would be able to heal itself or whether I would need an operation.

The stookie, from the top of my thigh down to my ankle, was really uncomfortable, but, for some reason, I felt OK and was confident that things were going to be fine. Part of the reason for my positive thinking was down to the fact that my dad had arrived from Bulgaria. I was so pleased to see him.

When I was lying in that hospital bed staring at the walls it was very depressing, but find me someone that is happy to be in hospital! At least that one was nice and clean. In Bulgaria the health system is poor, and they have next to no money to improve things. The hospitals are in a bad way: they have no air-conditioning and the smells aren't very nice, either.

Being in bed for such a long time gave me a chance to think about things, and I started to relive how the injury happened. I'm really superstitious, and as I thought about the incident, I began to realise that it could have something to do with McDiarmid Park. I came to believe that the stadium was cursed and that it was the cause of my leg break. It may sound far-fetched, but I have strong beliefs, and I vowed there and then that I'd never play at St Johnstone's ground again. My reasons would seem straightforward and natural to a Bulgarian, but many people in the world would find my superstitions a little bizarre.

Because of my superstitions, I stick to a rigid routine before every game. However, that night, for some reason, I broke my routine before and during the match, and I have no doubt it brought me bad luck by putting a curse on me. For example, I always tie my laces over the tongue of my boot, but, before the kick-off against St Johnstone, Henrik Larsson told me to put my tongue over my laces. I also changed my boots at half-time for the first time in my career. The biggest slice of bad luck came a couple of minutes before my injury occurred when one of the red and white laces that I wear around my wrist during games fell off. I always wear three of them because odd numbers bring good fortune in Bulgaria, and even numbers are bad luck. I couldn't find the one that had fallen off, and I had to play on with only two laces. That would be bad luck for anyone from Bulgaria. I knew it really wasn't my night when I had a goal chalked off, and minutes later, I clashed with Jim Weir and broke my leg. I decided in hospital that I had to protect myself in future, and I vowed there and then never to play at McDiarmid Park again.

In Bulgaria, superstitions are treated very seriously, and although some things may seem trivial to Westerners, I continue to do them. For example, I never accept a salt cellar directly from hand to hand: it has to be put down on the table before I can pick it up.

If Bulgarian people believe they are having a run of bad luck or suffer from phobias we have special people we can visit who help to take the bad luck away. I don't know what the equivalent would be over here, but I suppose the closest thing would be a witch doctor. They are freely available and live in the town just like normal people.

If my leg hadn't healed so quickly, or I had gone on a bad run of injuries, I'd have had no qualms about finding one of these special people in Bulgaria to help me to sort out my problems. Why not? I have always known how to locate them, but, thankfully, I did not need to do so.

When I was 11 years old I did have reason to visit one of these people because I suffered from a terrible fear of the wind. On gusty nights I used to be terrified that the buildings would collapse and people would be injured or killed. I'd hide under my covers for protection and pray the wind would cease.

My parents knew about my fears, and my mum decided that the only way to sort out my phobia was to take me to our local witch doctor. We kept it a secret from my dad because he wasn't in favour of them. The 'doctor' asked me what my problem was, and when I explained, she took me down to the river and brought out three bullets. She washed the bullets in the water, dried them and swirled them above my head. As she swirled the bullets around she chanted something to herself in a bid to get rid of my phobia. And it worked. It honestly did. I didn't feel any inner or outer body sensation during or after the event but obviously something happened. After that visit, I was never as frightened of the wind as I used to be, and I rarely think about it now.

Without the help of a Bulgarian 'doctor' I did play at McDiarmid Park again, in October of that year. I remember feeling really nervous before the game, and an hour before kick-off my heart was pumping like mad. The other players were aware of it and made a point of asking me if I was OK. I settled down in the first half and even had a hand in our first goal when Darren Dods headed my cross into his own net. They equalized but Henrik netted a last-minute free-kick, and after the game, I felt really good.

I knew I had overcome a huge psychological hurdle and felt like there was no looking back. The feeling was a million miles away from the one I had experienced the last time I'd played there. I was really proud of myself to have made it to that stage because my recovery was a long and, at times, tedious process.

It was a really difficult time for me but even harder for Paulina and my father. Dad stayed for almost a month, and he and Paulina had to put up with a lot. At times, they must have felt like chucking it all in and telling me where to go because I was ratty and would fly off the handle for no reason. I suppose I can put it down to being depressed about my injury. In many ways, the depression and anger was to be expected and was all part of the recovery process, but I hated being helpless. Thankfully, they understood and never complained.

Thank goodness they stood by me. I really needed them for so many things. If I woke during the night needing the toilet they would have to take turns to carry me to the loo. I also had to move my mattress down to the ground level of the apartment from our upstairs bedroom. I could no longer do the simplest things that I took for granted in everyday life, and I felt useless.

My Leg Break and Weird Superstitions

After a week, I returned to the hospital, and they told me that my leg hadn't set. As a result, they advised me to go through with the operation. It took just under an hour, and it went well. The next day, I couldn't believe it when the doctor told me I had to get out of bed and start to walk with crutches. I was worried because I didn't even think I'd be able to get myself out of bed, never mind walk. I told him I couldn't do it, but he forced me through the pain. I was almost crying with agony, but I had no choice other than to get on with it. It was the start of my recovery, and I was determined not to fall at the first hurdle.

Just two weeks later, Brian Scott told me to try walking without one of the crutches. I managed to do it, and the following week I got rid of the other one. I couldn't believe I was walking in that short space of time. I felt like a baby taking its first steps – it was a great feeling and a big relief.

My recovery went smoothly, and it wasn't long before I could do some light jogging. It hit me at that time that I was going to be able to walk down the aisle for my wedding on 9 June. When Brian Scott had told me shortly after the accident that I'd be sprinting down the aisle on my wedding day – which was about seven weeks away at that time – I had laughed at him. I didn't think it would be possible, but he was right, and on the morning of my wedding, I got out of bed and remembered his words. As a tribute to the Celtic medical staff, the management and my teammates, I took a quiet moment to reflect on what they had told me – I was glad that they were right and that I was ready for my big day.

Before my wedding day came around, I had my comeback public appearance in front of the Celtic fans when we won the league thanks to a Tommy Johnson goal in a 1–0 victory over St Mirren. I was delighted that we'd won the league, but it was hard to feel an important part of it, even though I had scored a few winning goals that season. I was pleased for the boys but would have loved to be out on the pitch when it was clinched. It's not the same when you're not playing.

When I was on the pitch to celebrate with the lads the whole occasion got to me. I had arrived at Celtic Park that afternoon and told myself that I wasn't going to cry and would behave normally, but I couldn't stop myself. When I walked onto the pitch my body was trembling, and I couldn't speak. I started crying for the first time in my life in response to anything to do with football. Paul Lambert came over to give me a big hug. He told me to enjoy the occasion and not to worry about my comeback.

The following week, the supporters again made me feel special when we beat Hearts 1–0 – Lubo Moravcik scoring a great goal – and were presented with the magnificent SPL championship trophy. The fans gave me a huge cheer when I stood on the podium in the middle of the park. Running around the pitch afterwards with the trophy was unbelievable – the players were all jumping about, singing and dancing, and the medical staff told me it was fine to join in. It was great to feel so happy again, and it was the first of many times in the space of a few weeks that I felt so elated.

Another happy occasion around that time was when I picked up the PFA Young Player of the Year award. Because I had missed the last couple of months of the season with the broken leg, I reckoned my chance had gone. I thought that St Johnstone's Keigan Parker or Dundee's Gavin Rae – who is now with Rangers – would win, and I was genuinely shocked to get the vote from my fellow pros. Henrik Larsson won the main award that night, and it topped off a great day for the club: we had beaten Rangers 3–0 at Ibrox that afternoon. Despite not taking much alcohol usually, I enjoyed a good few drinks that night, I can tell you.

We clinched the Treble against Hibs in the Scottish Cup final, having won the League Cup earlier in the year. That victory finished off the best season that the club had enjoyed in many years. In fact, it was Celtic's first Treble since 1969. I wasn't at Hampden for the Hibs game as I had travelled home to make all the last-minute arrangements for my wedding. On the day of the match, I had to go round the bars of Sofia to try to find a place that was showing the game. I eventually found one – an Irish bar full of Celtic fans – and settled down to watch the action. We won 3–0, and I felt really happy that the season had ended on a successful note. At the final whistle, all the Celtic fans offered to buy me drinks, and if I'd accepted every one of their offers, I'd have been drunk for a month. In the end, I had a couple but nothing over the top.

It was at that point that I started to feel a hint of anger, despite the fact that we'd just clinched the Treble. I thought back to that night at St Johnstone and how one moment had deprived me of the climax of the best season of my life. Rather than take a drink, I wanted to do something to help get rid of my frustration, but I couldn't think of anything that would make it better.

To get myself in a more positive frame of mind, I thought back to the time just after my leg break when we clinched the CIS League Cup with a 3–0 win over Kilmarnock. Just after the game Martin O'Neill and Jim Hone – Celtic's contract manager at the time – came round to my house with the cup to let me hold it. It was a lovely gesture matched by our first-team coach Steve Walford, who gave me his winner's medal from that day. It meant so much to me, and I'll always be grateful to him for that. Steve is an exceptional man, and I never heard any of the guys say a bad word about him, which is quite something when you think that he worked with about 30 players every day. He took me by surprise on the day he gave me his medal. A few of us were in the dressing-room and Steve asked for a bit of order and announced what he was doing, saying that I deserved the medal more than he did. I was really taken aback, and the boys clapped and cheered as I accepted it.

I think the heartache of my leg break finally vanished on the day I married Paulina Serafimova. The build-up to our big day always gave me something positive to focus on when I was down and depressed. I think that looking forward to our wedding was the catalyst for my recovery from my injury. It really helped me get back to fitness as early as I did.

We married in Sofia on a Saturday and it was broadcast live on national television, which was a big surprise to us. My international teammates came along and so did my good friend

Mark Burchill. Brian Wilson also attended, and I was pleased that the people that mattered most to me were there for the proudest day of my life.

On Bulgarian TV our marriage was billed as one of the celebrity events of the year, and although I wasn't too comfortable with that tag, I was also deeply proud. For the next few days, we were all over the celebrity pages of magazines and newspapers. Yes, I was a bit embarrassed by it all at the time, but after that day I felt like a new man. I was so happy.

Paulina is my best friend and my soul mate, and I knew from the moment we met I wanted to marry her. I can't ever imagine life without Paulina; it would destroy me if anything happened to her or Stiliyan, jun.

Paulina and I met in a restaurant in Bulgaria just before I left to join Celtic and then had to part because of my transfer. The fact we were so far apart might have killed off any chance we had, but we stuck at it and have a really strong relationship. We have experienced some tough times but have helped each other through them. She was always there for me at the end of the phone when I was going through my tough period with Celtic. I was homesick and had no money, but she told me to stick it out and it would all work out in the end.

We honeymooned in Bali and had a great time, but even on holiday, I continued to work my way back to fitness. I would get up at six every morning and go for a swim and a jog to build up my stamina and make sure I was in the best possible shape. Mind you, I don't think Paulina was too pleased that I neglected her on our honeymoon!

The other member of our family at the moment is our dog Chester. He's a right handful; you can't leave him alone for a minute. He's well behaved now, but when he was younger he got up to all sorts and, in the past, has chewed his way through my credit cards, my DVD system and a few £10 notes. We still love him to bits, though, and he's a great companion. I love to take him out for a long walk and just talk to him — I use him as a sort of soundboard and talk to him about football and the things I could be doing to improve my game. He obviously has no idea what I'm going on about, but I like doing it.

Chester was delighted to see us when we returned to Glasgow from our honeymoon early in July. It was about a week before pre-season was due to start, and I was bursting to get to the stadium and get started. In fact, I was so keen that I turned up at Parkhead one sunny morning before 6 a.m. because my body clock was still on Bali time. I had to get the security guard to open up and let me into the gym.

My recovery spiralled upwards from there, and before I knew it, I was joining in on full training sessions. I then played in a few reserve games and was happy to get stuck in and go for 50/50 balls. I knew I was ready for the real thing and kept on pestering the manager to play me. However, I knew he didn't want me to rush into anything, and I now understand that he was right. To be fair, I didn't have too long to wait, and, again, I have to thank Henrik for helping. Whenever I was down he was able to spot it a mile away because he had been through it all himself. He would often take time out to talk to me, and sometimes we'd sit together inside Parkhead with a glass of juice and discuss how I was feeling. It was so good to share things with him, and he was very understanding, always making sure that we finished the conversation on a positive note.

He knew all about the recovery process, the depression and the desperation to get back playing. He too had been made to bide his time, and I think it got to the stage that he begged Kenny Dalglish to give him a first-team game to prove he was properly fit again. Henrik got his wish when he came on as a sub against Dundee United at Parkhead in the last competitive game of the 1999–2000 season, and he received a standing ovation from the fans. A month later, he made it into the Sweden squad for the European Championships.

My wait was over when I started for Celtic on 8 September in a home game against Dunfermline, which we won 3–1 thanks to a double strike from Lubo Moravcik and a Chris Sutton goal.

You Can Call Me Stan

I played the full game, despite being a nervous man in the pre-match warm-up. I hardly slept a wink the night before, but our fans settled me down by chanting my name and they made me feel that I was ready to take on Dunfermline by myself. That was it: the 178-day nightmare that I had gone through since breaking my leg was over.

8

The Old Firm

Old Firm games are huge — the most special, exciting and nerve-racking 90 minutes any footballer will ever play. From the moment I signed for Celtic, the thing that kept being hammered home to me was the importance of beating Rangers. Jim Hone drummed that into me right from the off, telling me that Rangers had won just about everything for the last ten or eleven years. I quickly got used to that kind of talk as not a day went past when someone else didn't repeat the same thing.

I was told that games against Rangers have a special atmosphere on and off the pitch. Off the pitch it is unbelievable. The fans have a rivalry with each other that no two other clubs in the world have, and it's safe to say that some of it is not purely down to footballing reasons. Before joining the club, I had some idea of the kind of rivalry that there was between the two sets of supporters because I had watched Celtic and Rangers games on television. However, nothing could prepare me for the reality of the situation.

Being Bulgarian I find it hard to understand the whole Catholic and Protestant issue. There is nothing like it in my country and I'm quite grateful we're not affected by it, although I respect people's beliefs if they are practising them for the proper reasons. It's encouraging that in the past few years both clubs have made an effort to tackle the issue of sectarianism, and hopefully things will continue to improve. However, we still have a huge problem in the west of Scotland, and it's desperately sad to see that the rivalry has resulted in innocent people being attacked and murdered. That is totally wrong and can't be condoned or justified under any circumstances. When I've picked up a newspaper or watched television and heard about fights and other violence taking place before, during and after an Old Firm game it's made me feel sick. I hope that the effort that the fans put into backing their team on Old Firm day never changes, but it would be nice if the trouble was to cease, no matter how small the incidents might be.

I suppose the big positive side of the Old Firm's rivalry is that the fans give you so much backing during a game – it really helps you find an extra 5 per cent in your performance because you don't want to lose and have your nose rubbed in it for the next couple of weeks. Every Old Firm player feels the same. I have socialised with Rangers players and attended functions with them. We've got on well, and there is a healthy understanding between us because we know the pressures of being part of such huge clubs.

In particular, I have a lot of respect for former Ibrox captain Lorenzo Amoruso. He is a true leader on the pitch and the model professional off it. After I broke my leg, he took time out to call me to pass on his regards and the best wishes of the rest of the Rangers players. He didn't need to do it, but it indicates the kind of person that he is. He is the type of guy I'd be happy to have a beer with any day of the week. I was surprised Rangers sold him to Blackburn Rovers in the summer of 2003. He is a good defender and the kind of player we didn't like to face because he gave his heart and soul in every game and made sure his opponents knew they were in for a tough 90 minutes.

Stefan Klos is another Rangers player I admire. I don't really know him too well on a personal level, but he is a tremendous goalkeeper. He has saved Rangers on many occasions, and they are lucky to have him. Having a quality keeper is so important but they are not easy to find. Take Manchester United, for example. They have spent about £20 million trying to find a suitable replacement for the legendary Peter Schmeichel. Edwin van der Sar is the latest keeper to try and fill his gloves, but he has a tough job on his hands. Arsenal have found much the same problem trying to find a No. 1 with the talent and mental toughness to replace David Seaman.

Shota Arveladze was another impressive player for Rangers. Although he's left Ibrox now, I remember when he played for Ajax and scored against us in the Champions League. He caused us a lot of problems in those two legs, and I wasn't too pleased to hear he'd signed for Rangers. He is very quick, has good close control and is comfortable on either foot, which must make him a nightmare for defenders to mark. Shota wasn't around during my first season at Celtic, but Rangers still had plenty of quality in players like Jörg Albertz and Rod Wallace, a striker who could score from less than half a chance.

Predictably, there were plenty of incidents and controversy in the first Old Firm game that I played in on Sunday, 7 November 1999. Sadly, most of the things that happened that day I'd rather forget. The build-up to the match was intense, and it seemed that everyone in the country was talking about it. However, the main thing that I noticed in the lead-up to the derby was a little step up in pace in training. Everyone wanted to show the manager they were up for it and good enough to make an impact against Rangers.

Media coverage also intensifies, and there seems to be a greater demand to know what has been going on at the clubs ahead of the kick-off.

Despite warnings from experienced players such as Tom Boyd and Paul Lambert, nothing can prepare you for an Old Firm game. It is different from anything I've ever known, and I doubt there is anything to touch it. The games aren't always pretty, and for the purists, it must be, quite often, a total turn-off. That said, the matches are always eventful.

As I ran out of the Ibrox tunnel for my debut the noise was deafening, and I knew straight away what all the hype was about. The fans were mental. I was in a state of shock. Rangers took the lead through Jonatan Johansson, but we equalized through Eyal Berkovic, and, minutes later, he scored again with a fine individual goal to put us ahead. It was just what we wanted because we felt Rangers wouldn't be able to fight back, but it all went wrong right on the stroke of half-time when Paul Lambert fouled Albertz to concede a penalty. As if that wasn't enough, Paul had to be stretchered off as the Rangers player had landed on his face and knocked out a couple of the skipper's teeth and damaged his cheekbone.

Paul's an exceptional player, and the team just isn't the same without him. He gave tremendous protection to our defence, and his positional sense was different class. He would use his tactical awareness to great effect to break up opposition attacks. Of course, Paul has moved on now and has taken his first steps in management with Livingston, but the way he played for Celtic and the positive contribution he made to the club will be remembered for many years to come.

I'm sure Paul will do well at Livi. He worked hard in Germany to complete his coaching badges, and although the course he took on was an intensive one, he came through it with his already excellent reputation enhanced. He has won the Champions League and will be able to command the respect of any dressing-room in the world. I'm sure Paul will excel as a gaffer, but he will do well to prove he has the ability to be as successful a manager as he was a player. He is a gentleman and one of the best professionals you will ever come across.

So, you can appreciate how much of a blow it was to lose Paul in that game. The Rangers players wanted him sent off, but I think referee Kenny Clark was right to ignore their claims. Albertz scored the penalty to make it 2–2 and gave Rangers a lift going into the break. That really deflated us, and I have often wondered what might have happened in that game if we had held out until half-time.

Still, with a guy like Albertz in their side, they were always going to cause us problems. I always admired him, but it wasn't until I played against him that I realised just how tough he was and how good a player. He could win games for Rangers. He had the physical strength to knock opponents over, and his thunderous shot was almost powerful enough to blast keepers through the net. I have to say, he is the most difficult opponent I have played against in domestic football in Scotland, and I was delighted, and surprised, when Dick Advocaat sold him back to Hamburg. A big mistake. I can't pay Albertz a bigger compliment.

Amoruso and Gabby Amato scored for Rangers in the second half, and that was game over. We lost 4–2. I had a nightmare that day. For a start, I didn't expect to play from the beginning of the match, but John Barnes announced the team on the morning of the game and told me I was playing on the left-hand side of midfield. It was a position that I wasn't used to and was totally uncomfortable with. I might have felt better if he had come to me to explain his decision and talk me through what he wanted, but there was no communication. I had a dozen questions that I wanted to ask, but no one from the management team was there to answer them.

When the boss announced what position I would be playing, I thought to myself, 'Oh, my God, what am I going to do?' Not the ideal frame of mind to be in as you are walking out for your first game against Rangers! Every time I got the ball I was terrified of making a mistake. I don't think I passed the ball more than two yards. It got even worse when I was moved to left-back. Well, I don't need to tell you that Sergio Porrini and Claudio Reyna both had a field day against me. They had the cigars out, and I must have made them look like Brazilian world-beaters. I reckon that with my performance I'd guaranteed them a starting place for the next three months. I was subbed for Regi Blinker after about an hour, and normally I would have been extremely disappointed to be taken off. But I was happy to get the tracksuit on that day, something I'm not proud to admit. I had to forget that game quickly, but it was difficult when Brian Wilson kept slaughtering my performance and telling me that I'd be chased out of Glasgow if I didn't start improving.

The next Old Firm game was just before the end of the year at Parkhead, and we had to win it to have a chance of lifting the title. A defeat would have been the end of our championship dream. The game finished 1–1, and even with that point, I think we knew it was going to take a minor miracle to catch Rangers and win the league. We dominated and took the lead through Mark Viduka when he scored with a low shot from the edge of the box past Lionel Charbonnier.

Rangers came back into the game before we had a chance to settle and frustrate them, equalizing thanks to a Billy Dodds goal. It went from bad to worse after that. The next game was at Parkhead in March. Kenny Dalglish and Tommy Burns were in charge for that match, after John Barnes and Eric Black had been sacked. It was a cold and wet night, and we really battered Rangers but just couldn't put the ball in the net. Klos was in great form, but we missed a couple of sitters. Before we knew it, we were hit by a classic sucker punch. Wallace scored a goal in the final minutes to give them the points that all but wrapped up the championship for them for the second season in a row.

The next derby match was the worst ever. It was a game I would rather not have had to play in because, at that time, they played like a team who knew they had the edge over us. They knew they were going to beat us before a ball was kicked, and we could do nothing about it. We were humbled 4–0 that Sunday afternoon in March. To make it worse, midway through the second half they started showboating, spraying the ball about the pitch as their fans chanted '*Ole!*' There's almost nothing worse for a footballer to hear than that. It made me really angry, and it was difficult to keep a sane head. The best way to hit back would have been to have scored a couple of goals, but we couldn't manage that. We were hopeless and pathetic and deserved to lose by that margin.

After the game, the Rangers players said they were angry with comments that Johan Mjällby had made in a newspaper on the morning of the match. He had said that Celtic had better players than Rangers and that we could beat them on our day. We certainly didn't show it that afternoon! But I was proud of Johan's comments. He just wanted to fight back because he was frustrated at Rangers being ahead of us in the league. He was the type of player that every team needed. Johan never let his head go down; he never gave up, and he scared the life out of opposition attackers. I was sorry to see the big Swede leave in the summer of 2004, but he was made a very good offer to go and play in Spain with Levante and couldn't be blamed for taking on a new challenge in the excellent Spanish *Primera Liga* so late in his career.

I was scared that day and remember asking Paul Lambert after the game if our supporters would come back to see us play the next season. He told me that they would as they were a loyal bunch and that the best way to pay them back was to go on and win the league that season. I was not convinced, to be honest. In fact, I reckoned Paul had lost the plot, although, at that time, I kept my thoughts to myself! However, one game into the new season, the stadium was full as usual, and a year later, Paul's prediction came true.

A couple of weeks into the season, big Johan's prophetic words also came true. We won the first Old Firm game of the 2000–01 season with Martin O'Neill in charge, and I'm glad to say we clinched it in style. Before the game, I had felt a sense of optimism in our camp. The manager seemed to be in a positive frame of mind, and it looked to me as though he thought we were definitely going to win. The way he was behaving must have rubbed off on the players. Well, it certainly rubbed off on me, anyway.

It was my first win against Rangers in five attempts, and it was worth the wait. A 6–2 victory – brilliant. I even managed to score. Chris Sutton netted the first, then I scored the second when I managed to lose my marker Fernando Ricksen at a corner kick and head home into the net. I couldn't believe it and didn't even know how to celebrate. I just went crazy and celebrated in front of the Rangers fans. In hindsight, it was not the wisest thing to do, and, unsurprisingly, they weren't too happy about it!

Paul Lambert then made it 3–0, and there were only 15 minutes on the clock! Claudio Reyna gave Rangers a glimmer of hope of getting back into the game with a goal on the 40-minute mark, and shortly before half-time, they had a goal disallowed. But, in the second half, we came to life again, and Henrik Larsson scored two fabulous goals to put us 5–1 up. It was fairy-tale stuff.

They scored from a Billy Dodds penalty, but we had the last laugh when Sutty slid home the sixth from Stéphane Mahé's cross. Barry Ferguson was sent off near the end of the game for his second yellow card to make it a miserable day all round for him and his club.

I like Barry and rate him highly as a footballer. He's young, has a great touch, great awareness and can hit a lovely pass. He also scores goals now, and that is important for a midfielder in his position. I know it isn't safe for players to cross the Old Firm divide and move from one club to the other, but I think Barry would be worth the risk for Celtic. However, I have to be honest and say that there's no chance of him ever becoming the modern-day Mo Johnston.

When Barry moved to Blackburn Rovers in a deal worth around £6.5 million, I think it was money well spent by the English side. He left Rangers because he wanted to test himself in one of the best leagues in the world, but I'm surprised he didn't stay in the Premiership longer. Rangers will be happy they've got their captain back, but it's not such good news for Celtic, because he has the potential to become a world-class performer. Joining Celtic must have been the last thing on Barry's mind as he made the long and lonely walk across the pitch, receiving dog's abuse from our fans.

Barry probably left Rangers in the first place because he knew that the level of competition wasn't strong enough in the SPL. Look at Paul Lambert. He had to leave and play in Germany for Borussia

Dortmund before earning the deserved reputation he has now. Paul has told me that he learned so much in the Bundesliga about football, especially in terms of having the discipline to play in a position and not wander during a game. He also absorbed the importance of preparation for a match.

The 6–2 game mentally and physically exhausted me, and I took cramp with ten minutes to go. I put so much into that game, but it was well worth it. After the final whistle, our dressing-room was like a big party. Everyone was shouting, and there was a really happy atmosphere. It made a pleasant change for our dressing-room to be noisy for the right reasons.

That game really helped me to feel like a part of it all. It was the first time I had played in a winning team against Rangers, and it felt special. I have since also realised that it was the day my good relationship with the Celtic fans was cemented. They have for the most part been good to me, but that game bolstered the bond between us. I helped to give them something to smile about, and when you do that, you remain in their hearts forever.

I must have also made an impression on the Rangers fans because two of them came up to me at Glasgow Airport the next day to congratulate me on my performance. I appreciated that and have always had a good relationship with the supporters of our greatest rivals. I have never had a problem with them, and that episode showed they appreciate good football.

The 6–2 match will live with me forever. Martin O'Neill also loved every minute of it. It helped him settle in right away and sent out the signals to everyone that he was the man who was going to do the business for Celtic. It gave us the belief that we were capable of winning the league, and, of course, nine months later we did.

Martin O'Neill didn't look back from that day onwards. On the other hand, I reckon that was the beginning of the end for Dick Advocaat as manager of Rangers. It gave the Ibrox men a warning that we meant business and had the mentality and ability to end their domination. They couldn't respond to the challenge.

It took another 15 months before Dick chucked it to move

upstairs and Alex McLeish came in. I think Advocaat was a very good coach for Rangers, I want to make that clear, but he was probably right to walk away when he did. He had tried to prove he was the best in the country but, ultimately, couldn't get the better of our manager. When his team couldn't beat us the Rangers supporters started putting pressure on him. The intensity of being an Old Firm boss under that level of scrutiny can't be easy to live with. When John Barnes was our manager he had the same problem against Advocaat and had to go.

Rangers did manage to beat us 5–1 in the next derby match to put them back in with a shout of winning the league. Brian Wilson was in a foul mood after that display and gave me pelters for not doing enough in the 90 minutes. I don't mind criticism; I can take it. Anyway, I have no choice when he is in the mood for letting off steam. I'm sure all the Celtic fans felt the same and must hate losing to Rangers as much as the players do.

I have tried to erase that day from my memory and can only remember the basic facts, like Ferguson gave them the lead and enjoyed celebrating to the full, probably feeling relieved after what had happened to him in the last Old Firm game. Henrik equalized, but it wasn't enough. Rangers scored four more thanks to Tore André Flo – who was making his debut after his £12 million transfer from Chelsea – Lorenzo Amoruso, Ronald de Boer and Michael Mols. Once again, it was a sore one for us and a reminder that Rangers wouldn't give up their league title without a fight. Obviously, our dressing-room was like a morgue after that defeat. Martin O'Neill wasn't happy with the result, but made sure he kept his after-match team-talk as positive as possible. He told us to get our heads back up immediately and make sure that the result didn't break us. We drew 0–0 against Hibs at Easter Road three days later on a really windy night. It was a decent point for us to get in those conditions and stopped the rot before a losing streak could get going.

The 5–1 defeat was the last time that the Rangers fans could afford a smile after playing us that season. We subsequently played them three more times and won every time. We beat them in the CIS Cup semi-final at Hampden 3–1 – Henrik and Sutty got the goals between them. Alan Thompson scored the only goal when we edged past them 1–0 at Parkhead in the next game, and that just about clinched the title for us.

I didn't play in the last Old Firm game of the season because of my broken leg but watched the match on TV at my house as we went to Ibrox and thumped them 3–0. We absolutely slaughtered Rangers that day, and it was perfect revenge for the 4–0 defeat on their ground a year earlier. Lubo was magnificent that afternoon and took the mickey out of them. He scored two goals, and Henrik got the other. It was a perfect time and place for him to score his 50th goal of the season. I remember watching him celebrate in front of the Broomloan Stand and wanted to jump through the telly and swap places with him.

We went on to win the league by 15 points that season. It was a winning margin to be proud of, although some fans were disappointed that we didn't win by more than 21 points – the amount by which Rangers had won the previous season. Of course, it would have been nice to do that, but winning the league was the most important thing. It was only the second time that Celtic had won the title in 12 years, and it was always our priority at the start of that season. Anything else, like the amount of points that we won by, was no more than a bonus.

We started off well in the 2001–02 season, winning the first two Old Firm games of the season. The first was a 2–0 win at Ibrox when I scored the opening goal with one of my free-kick specials, although Stefan Klos might have felt that he should have saved it. Alan Thompson scored a beauty right on the final whistle to deservedly give us the three points. In that match, Henrik also missed a penalty, and Lorenzo Amoruso was sent off. A red card in every Old Firm game seemed to be normal.

At that time, a popular opinion was that we were beating Rangers but didn't really deserve to be doing so. We felt that was a harsh assessment and wanted to prove it against them in the next game at Parkhead. We won 2–1 thanks to goals from Joos Valgaeren and Henrik Larsson. They got one back through Peter Lovenkrands, but it wasn't enough. I also remember Michael Ball and Dick Advocaat had an argument on the touchline after the full-back had been subbed. Ball had a right go at Advocaat, and I couldn't believe it.

Once again, despite the fact that we had won, Rangers felt that they were hard done by. I accept that they played good football, but the most important thing in the game is scoring goals. Football is all about the end product, and the team that puts the ball in the net deserves the credit. I was getting a bit fed up listening to the hard-luck stories by that point. Sometimes defeat just has to be accepted for what it is; it's better to say nothing rather than offer excuses.

We played them again that season in the semi-final of the CIS Cup, and they beat us 2–1. It was McLeish's first Old Firm game, and he couldn't have wished for a better start. When our paths crossed again in the league at Ibrox, I scored the opener, but Rangers came back to level the match with a sensational goal from Arthur Numan. Numan is another person I admire and respect. He is a gentleman off the park and an excellent professional on it. Again, I was really surprised when Rangers couldn't give him the deal that he wanted, and he retired from football in the summer of 2003. I don't think he has ever been properly replaced, which is great news for us.

The last league encounter that season came at Celtic Park in April and we had already won the title by that stage. It finished 1–1 and three players – John Hartson, Johan Mjällby and Fernando Ricksen – were sent off in the last minute. However, it wasn't a dirty game, and I thought they were all quite unlucky to see red. Thankfully, Hartson later won an appeal against the decision with a little help from Rangers' Bob Malcolm, who had come to the defence of our player. I know big John and the rest of the boys appreciated that gesture.

Our final meeting of that season was in the Scottish Cup final on

4 May 2002. The game was nicely set up as we were going for the Double and Rangers were going for a cup Double. Something had to give, and, sadly, we lost 3–2. We had no complaints as Rangers were the better team on the day. I really don't know what happened to us: we just didn't have it in us for one last push, and we lost to a Peter Lovenkrands goal in the final seconds after twice taking the lead through John Hartson and Bobo Balde.

After a long and exhausting season I really needed a rest and enjoyed a nice holiday with Paulina in Mexico. We had a great time. We went swimming with dolphins, which was a great experience. During the holiday, I kept thinking back to the Cup final, questioning whether we could have changed anything to get the right result. But, in the end, I had to accept that Rangers had played well. McLeish had made a difference to their side. They now played like a team and fought for each other: important ingredients that might have been missing towards the end of Advocaat's reign. We knew from that day on that we had a battle on our hands to remain the top team in the country, and if we weren't up for it, we would suffer.

McLeish is also a good coach, and he proved that much when he was at Hibs. He helped them to qualify for Europe and took them to a Scottish Cup final. He didn't win a trophy but might well have done had Hibs been in a position financially to keep their best players like Didier Agathe and Kenny Miller. I know some Rangers fans weren't happy when McLeish was appointed because they wanted a big name like Louis van Gaal or George Graham, but I think the board made the right choice. Alex brought much-needed fight to the team as well as passion, hunger and motivation. All these ingredients are required if a team is to win the league.

It also helps if there are no external distractions. One such distraction in recent years has been the talk of Celtic and Rangers moving to the English Premiership. Any chance of this happening appears to have disappeared for now. I am happy about that – for the moment. Celtic play in Scotland and are a Scottish club. It is important for them to keep their identity, but I think change is a must. For a while, I was optimistic that the game in Scotland was improving and that competition was getting stronger, with the likes of Aberdeen, Hibs, Motherwell and Hearts showing positive signs. Although these teams have no money to spend on players, they have been performing fairly well and have brought through some quality kids.

However, in the long run I don't think that the progress made by other teams is enough. We play each other too often and sometimes the excitement is missing when you get out of bed on the morning of a game. That's not a good sign; it's a worrying sign. I accept that change in Scotland is going to happen – perhaps even within the next five years – but I have mixed emotions about it. Yes, the thought of playing at Old Trafford, Highbury and Anfield on a regular basis is exciting, and I have no doubt we would do well. On our day, we're a match for any club in Britain, and the results we've had down south in challenge matches against Manchester United, Arsenal and Spurs have been encouraging. However, a part of me thinks that we might not win a trophy down there for a while. It's hard enough to win something in Scotland, never mind in England playing against the sides that they have down there, especially away from home. It could possibly take us two or three years to really find our feet, and if we could qualify for Europe within that timescale, it would be a major achievement.

I know that money would roll in from television and advertising, which would keep the board happy, but once the novelty of visiting the grounds of the major clubs wore off, our fans might not like the idea of us winning only around 70 per cent of our games when they have been used to winning at least 90 per cent in Scotland. The players and management would feel the same way.

Being part of a season-long midweek European league has also been mentioned, and I like the idea of that. It would keep us playing against top-class opposition on a regular basis. However, we have to get on with what we've got, and I'm not too disappointed change isn't happening right away, but I do want change eventually as playing each other five or six times a season can sometimes be boring.

Being in Scotland has been good for Celtic, and it's always worked out for the best. It is now vitally important that everyone in this country works hard to make our league better and that all clubs receive funds to improve their training grounds and to buy better players to boost the level of competition. Also, Scottish football is not as bad as some like to make out. I am proud to be part of it, and know I will feel that way for many years to come. If change comes, I will accept it and get on with it. The most important thing is that I'm still playing for Celtic if it happens.

Games against Rangers definitely keep me going, and I look forward to them so much. After losing the 2002 Cup final to our greatest rivals we wanted revenge as quickly as possible the following season and came up against them on 6 October at Parkhead. The game finished 3–3, and we were absolutely gutted not to have won. I have to say, Ronald de Boer had a fantastic game for Rangers that day, making things happen for the rest of his teammates. He was involved when they took an early lead, finding Mikel Arteta with a pass, the Spaniard firing past Rab Douglas. We should never have conceded that goal.

Gradually, we took a hold of the midfield, and our superiority finally paid dividends. Stefan Klos made a good save from one of my efforts but had no answer when Henrik controlled a cross from Momo Sylla and turned almost full circle to batter the ball home. Henrik was at it again to put us in the lead, getting on the end of a Thompson corner to head in. De Boer wasn't finished yet, scoring himself to make it 2–2, and then Arveladze netted to put Rangers in the lead. We couldn't believe that we were behind, but we came back to equalize – Chris Sutton scoring the goal – and were more than worthy of a point. Unfortunately, it wasn't quite good enough as Rangers stayed top of the league after that result. They had quality players like de Boer and Arteta, but we knew we were the better team.

The next Old Firm game was a chance for us to prove our

superiority, but things didn't work out as we had wished. The game at Ibrox on 7 December 2002 was another thrilling encounter and it served as a wake-up call to us as Rangers extended their lead at the top of the table. However, we didn't deserve to leave Ibrox empty handed, and the fact Stefan Klos was named Man of the Match gives an indication as to how we played. We did take the lead that day with the fastest ever goal recorded in an Old Firm game when Chris Sutton scored after just 18 seconds. Before that, Ally McCoist had held the record, scoring after just 40 seconds in a game at Parkhead in 1983. But we couldn't hold onto our flying start, and Rangers went in at half-time with a 3–1 lead after goals from Craig Moore, Ronald de Boer and Michael Mols.

John Hartson pulled one back for us after the break, but it wasn't enough. We pounded Klos's goal but had no luck, and he pulled off a couple of great stops. It was the first time we had lost to Rangers in the league for 25 months, the last time being the day that they hammered us 5–1. It was a sore one, and we were really hurt by the loss. It also meant that we had gone six games without wining an Old Firm derby, and that was far from acceptable.

We felt a lot of pressure going into the next game against Rangers on 8 March 2003 and knew we had to respond. It was in the middle of a hectic month in which we were going to face them again in the final of the CIS League Cup and play Liverpool over two legs in the UEFA Cup quarter-final. At that time, the popular line of questioning was 'If you only had one victory out of the three games which one would you prefer?' Well, as a footballer you want to win every game, and we were determined to beat Rangers in the two games and knock out Liverpool as well.

The old cliché of taking one game at a time is often used, but it was definitely an outlook we required at that particular time. Knowing that we hadn't won an Old Firm game in any of the previous six encounters and the fact that McLeish had yet to lose to Celtic since taking over as the Rangers manager was getting to us, and we had to do something about it.

We battered them that day, and the only surprise was how long it took for us to score. We netted on 57 minutes thanks to a fantastic right-foot finish from Hartson, although we could have scored more. I remember being really chuffed for big Rab that day, as he pulled off a great save in the final minutes from an Amoruso thunderbolt to make sure we held on. Rab had been criticised for some of the goals that he had lost to Rangers in previous games, but he bounced back to play a massive part in that win. I was also pleased for big John because with Henrik out injured at that time with a broken jaw, there was extra pressure on him to come up with the goods, and he managed the perfect response.

However, John suffered the agony of missing a penalty in his next Old Firm game – the CIS League Cup final on 16 March – and it just proves the point that it doesn't do any harm to expect the unexpected in games between Celtic and Rangers. Rangers were two ahead by half-time, their goals coming from Claudio Caniggia and Peter Lovenkrands. At that time, Lovenkrands seemed to be able to score every time he played against us, and we had trouble coping with his pace and movement.

I was left on the bench for that final and was bitterly disappointed not to make it. I hate missing out on any games, especially against our greatest rivals. With a few minutes remaining, I came on for Johan Mjällby, but there wasn't enough time to really get involved. We were down to ten men by that stage – Neil Lennon having been sent off after receiving two yellow cards – and we also had Sutton stretchered off after he collided with Bobo Balde at a corner.

We had pulled a goal back by that point, Henrik having headed home a Thompson corner. We were all over them, and it was the usual stuff from Klos as he denied us time after time. The linesman also denied us a good goal from Hartson that would have made it 2–2. He flagged for offside, but John was clearly onside when the pass was made. With time running out, Kenny Clark awarded us a penalty after Bobo was brought down by Amoruso. Hartson stepped up but put his spot-kick wide, and the cup was on its way to Ibrox. That was their first step towards winning the Treble that season. As I left Hampden that day, I didn't think for a minute that they would go on to achieve such a feat.

We only had to wait until 27 April to play Rangers again in the league, at a time when we were trailing them by eight points. There was more than the usual controversy surrounding the match as we had to play it only about 60 hours after we had returned from Boavista, where our stunning 1–0 victory had secured us a place in the UEFA Cup final. Quite rightly, we felt that the match could have been put back a day or so, or even just a few hours from the lunchtime kick-off to give us a little extra rest after doing ourselves and Scottish football proud, but the authorities were having none of it. So, we were knackered going into the game. Regardless of how tired I was, I was disappointed to have been named as a substitute by the gaffer when I so desperately wanted to play.

Our fans were in a party mood that day, and they spurred us on to a 2–1 success in a game that we had to win to keep the title race alive. Seeing our fans with their sombreros on and throwing beach balls around was entertaining, and it gave us all a lift. There's no doubt that the backing from the fans that day inspired us to win the three points. In saying that, no matter what the score was in that match, our supporters were going to feel superior to their Rangers counterparts as Celtic had a European final to look forward to. That was always going to be the main focus of the fans' attention in the closing weeks of the season.

The manager brought in Jackie McNamara and Ulrik Laursen to play from the start, but O'Neill's plans suffered a setback with just eight minutes played when Rab limped off with a thigh strain and had to be replaced by Javier Sanchez-Broto. Javier was obviously nervous coming off the bench for such a huge game but performed really well. Jackie, who skippered us that day, and Ulrik were both solid in their full-back roles.

Rangers started well and could have scored three goals inside the first fifteen minutes. We kept our cool, though, and won a penalty when Amoruso body checked Hartson: Alan Thompson was deadly from the spot. After taking an early pounding it was

My first ball, and even when I
was four my brother Ivan
couldn't get it off me!

It's playtime in the Petrov
house as Ivan and I go for
a ride on a rocking horse.

Getting ready to blow out the candles
on my fifth birthday cake.

My 40th day in the Bulgarian Army, swearing allegiance to my country.

I love representing Bulgaria and consider captaining my country as one of my greatest achievements in the game to date.

My first Celtic jersey as John Barnes proudly parades me to the media. The next few months were a disaster for us both.

The night in October 1999 when it all became too much for me. Kevin Twaddle scores the winner at Parkhead as my Celtic career lurches from one disaster to another.

It's bedlam at Celtic Park as I head home the second goal on our way to an unbelievable 6–2 Old Firm win in August 2000. It was Martin O'Neill's first game against Rangers.

Although I look calm, I'm in agony as Doc Roddy and Brian Scott confirm my worst fears that I've broken my leg at McDiarmid Park.

Despite the fact that I was in the middle of my recovery from a broken leg this was an unforgettable night for me and Celtic. After beating Rangers 3–0 at Ibrox that afternoon, Henrik accepts his 2000–01 Player of the Year award, and I pick up the Young Player of the Year honour.

One of the happiest days of my life as Paulina and I tie the knot in 2001 in Bulgaria.

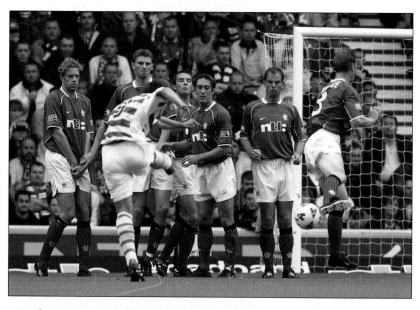

Goals against our biggest rivals are extra special, and this one against Rangers in our 2–0 win at Ibrox in September 2001 was particularly memorable.

Our charity night for young cerebral palsy sufferer Ilyan Bakalov was a huge success. Giving their support to our cause are Paulina, Momo Sylla, John Hartson, Elaine C. Smith, Bobo Balde and Lubo Moravcik.

It's two in a row as I lift the 2001–02 SPL trophy with Paul Lambert.

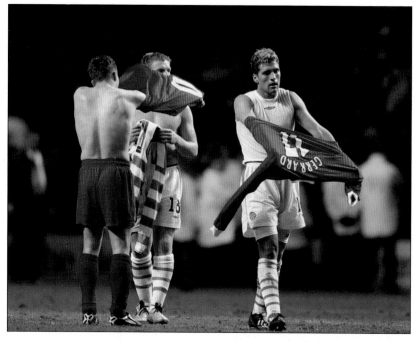

On the road to Seville in 2003. I swap shirts with Steven
Gerrard at the end of our home game against Liverpool.

Pain is written all over my face as I walk off the
pitch with Martin O'Neill in Seville after
the 2003 UEFA Cup final against Porto.

Paulina and I share a tender moment with young Stiliyan a couple of weeks after he was born in February 2003.

Young Stiliyan wearing his first Celtic strip. I'd be happy if he wore it for real one day.

Another trophy for Celtic as I slide home the third in our 3–1 cup final win against Dunfermline at Hampden in May 2004. It was Henrik's last game for the club.

A night I'd rather forget as we troop off the pitch in misery
after our 5–0 Champions League hammering in Bratislava.

We love going back to Montana in the summer, and here
Paulina and I are joined by my father, Stiliyan, jun.,
mum and brother Ivan.

fantastic to be a goal ahead at that stage, and our fans went crazy. I warmed up in front of them and will never forget the sight of them in their Spanish get-ups. We were two up before half-time when Big Bad John scored another great Old Firm goal. Although Rangers grabbed a lifeline on 57 minutes thanks to a strike from Ronald de Boer, we never felt like they had enough to take a point off us. I came on for big John on the 66-minute mark and can recall being clattered by Craig Moore, a challenge that earned him a yellow card from referee Hugh Dallas.

At the end of that game, we knew we were right back in the league hunt, and despite thinking about the UEFA Cup final, we managed to claw back the points difference over the final handful of games to set up a nail-biting final day of the SPL season on 25 May. We were second on goal difference going into that final Sunday. Amazingly, it was so tight that we were both 68 goals to the good on goal difference, but Rangers were in pole position as they had scored one more than us.

They started the day as favourites because they were at home to Dunfermline, and we had to travel to Kilmarnock. By the end of the afternoon, our fears had come true: Rangers had hammered Dunfermline 6–1, and we only managed a 4–0 win at Rugby Park. We were two up at half-time thanks to a double from Chris Sutton, but Rangers were 3–1 ahead at the same point. We went top of the table when an Alan Thompson penalty on fifty-four minutes put us further in front, but our joy lasted less than ten minutes as Ronald de Boer scored another for Rangers. I netted a fourth then Thompson missed a penalty. I'm glad that spot-kick miss wasn't the difference between us winning and losing the league as it would have been totally unfair to have that hanging around Alan's shoulders.

To this day, I still can't properly put into words how I felt that afternoon about the way our season ended. In March we were in the running for four trophies and ended up with nothing. It was no reflection on our efforts that season, and we didn't deserve to finish empty handed. Every player, each member of the management and all the backroom staff put so much effort into trying to get things right, but, one by one, the trophies were taken away from us. We lost to Rangers in the CIS Cup final then Inverness knocked us out of the Scottish Cup. Porto beat us in the cruellest of circumstances in the UEFA Cup final, and just when we thought nothing would top that, we lost our league title to Rangers on goal difference.

I have to be honest and admit that I didn't have a good feeling going into that final league game. I was confident we would take care of Kilmarnock but always felt Rangers would score as many goals as they were going to need against Dunfermline, and that turned out to be the case.

I was gutted. Heartbroken. Call it what you like. For that to happen to us just five days after losing the UEFA Cup final was so cruel and unfair. Our dressing-room was silent after the league decider, and I've never seen so many grown men look as deflated as our guys did that day.

I was distraught when I left Rugby Park that night. To be honest, I couldn't believe we had finished the season with nothing to show for our efforts, and the feeling of emptiness took a couple of weeks to sink in. It was even more disappointing because we never got the chance to thank our fans for their support throughout the season. In particular, they deserved credit for the way that they had supported us in our run to the UEFA Cup final, following us on our journey around Europe. Approximately 80,000 of them travelled to Seville for the final against Porto, which was truly amazing. The reception that they gave us that night was incredible, as it was down at Kilmarnock the day we lost the league.

I remember sitting with Paulina one day during our holiday in Greece and thinking out loud. I said to her that I wished that I had sampled the feeling of running round the stadium in Seville with the UEFA Cup in my hands. If we had won the trophy that night what kind of reception would we have received? I reckon some of our supporters would still be there partying now if we'd beaten

Porto! I also wondered what kind of reception we'd have received if we'd managed to win the league at Kilmarnock. Again, we received a great response from our supporters, but imagine what it would have been like if we'd won the championship on the last day. I know that it's all hypothetical; it is all behind us now. We have all moved on. However, as much as I was gutted not to win anything, the memories of Seville and beating Liverpool at Anfield and Blackburn at Ewood Park are the best feelings that I have ever had in this game.

It was a strange sensation that summer not being the champions of Scotland. It was horrible, really. I'm just glad there was no football to be played that summer, and I went away for a nice break with my family to Greece and switched off for a few weeks. I was mentally and physically exhausted after that season, and when I think about it now, I still can't believe there wasn't a medal to show for our efforts. I'm sure that if we had not have had the UEFA Cup to think about that season we would have won the league because we were the best team in Scotland. Sadly, the record books won't show that. I hope that doesn't sound disrespectful to Rangers, it's just my honest opinion. Deep down, if the people at Rangers are honest, I'm sure they would agree they were fortunate to win the title in 2003, and being out of Europe from an early stage that season meant they had nothing else but domestic football to concentrate on.

When you feel you've suffered an injustice you want to put it right as quickly as possible, but we had to wait until 4 October for our next game against Rangers. We visited Ibrox for the match in good spirits after a good midweek win against Lyon in the Champions League. However, we had a few injury problems for the game, and Chris Sutton had to play in the centre of defence alongside Stan Varga. Both of them were absolutely superb. Chris is one of the most complete footballers I've ever come across, and whether he plays as a striker, a central midfielder or a defender, he is always a stand-out performer.

As solid as Sutton was in defence, Hartson was as prolific up front and scored the only goal of the game less than a minute into the second half. The big man got up to flick a long ball on to Henrik, who then played his strike partner back in. John's effort from a wide angle inside the box took a deflection off the foot of Zurab Khizanishvili and looped over the head of Stefan Klos. It was John's 50th goal for Celtic, and despite hitting the Rangers player on the way in, there was no way that he would let it be given as an own goal.

The three points took us to the top of the league for the first time that season, and Rangers just couldn't compete with us that afternoon. Too many of their players didn't look hungry enough, and they seemed to lack the desire needed for Old Firm games. We never looked back and believed from that day on that we were going to win the title back.

By the time we played Rangers again, we were already eight points ahead in the league. The game took place at Parkhead on 3 January, and we knew a win would see the SPL trophy back in its rightful place. I was really up for that game and teamed up with Didier Agathe on the right-hand side. We didn't allow Michael Ball to get going and made sure he stayed in his own half. He was keeping a close watch on me but let his guard down when I managed to escape him a few minutes into the match to put us ahead. Henrik crossed from the left, and I timed my run to the back post to get on the end of it with a diving header. The ball somehow managed to crawl over the line after Klos had touched it onto his right-hand post, and it rolled along the line before going in off the opposite post. I was thrilled by that goal, I really was.

Once again, we dominated and played Rangers off the park. We scored two more to win by an emphatic margin. Varga made it 2–0 after 58 minutes with a powerful header, and Thompson scored with a great free-kick from 25 yards out to give a true reflection of the balance of play. It meant that with just 19 league games played, we were already 11 points ahead of Rangers and cruising to the title. That win was also our 18th straight victory in the SPL. We were all proud of that statistic as it beat the record held by Jock Stein's Lisbon Lions side from 1968. The only slight disappointment that day was that John Hartson failed to find the net. He had scored in the previous four Old Firm games and one that day would have given him the honour of being the first ever Rangers or Celtic player to score in five consecutive Glasgow derby games.

When we next took on Rangers on 28 March we were well on our way to the title and, once again, arrived at Ibrox on the back of another excellent European result. The fans had their sombreros and beach balls out again as we had just returned four days earlier from a fantastic 0–0 draw in the Nou Camp that had knocked Barcelona out from the UEFA Cup and set up a quarter-final clash against another Spanish side, Villarreal.

Despite being knackered from our exertions in Spain, we defeated Rangers 2–1, and by beating them five times in a row in the league we set a new club record. We had taken the lead in the first half. Gavin Rae fouled me out on the left, and Thommo had swung over an inviting free-kick. Henrik was first to react and made his way in between a couple of static Rangers defenders to head into the net. It was a terrific start and also the 20th game in a row that we had managed to find a way past the Rangers defence – a record that stretched back to Martin O'Neill's first Old Firm game in August 2000 when we won 6–2.

We didn't quite manage to beat Stefan Klos six times, but we did score again thanks to a tap-in from Alan Thompson after Klos had parried a Stephen Pearson shot. The only blip came when Stevie Thompson scored with a header from a Chris Burke corner to give them their first goal against us in four matches. I have to say I rate young Burke. He has good skill and is a player we always make sure we keep a close eye on when we face Rangers. I'm sure he has a great future at the highest level.

Although Burke seems to be a confident player, I detected a real lack of confidence from Rangers when we were up against them during that period. We seemed to believe we could beat them every time we met them, and I could sense they knew it. There's no doubt we went into those games brimming with confidence, and you could sense Rangers were scared of us at set pieces. We always felt we could score when we had a corner or a cross from a wide area. If we netted first, we knew they probably wouldn't have the strength of character or the necessary belief to come back and win.

The last Old Firm clash of the 2003–04 season was a home game for us on 8 May. We went into it knowing that if we won it we'd have managed a clean sweep of all four league clashes that season. It was also Henrik's last Old Firm game and we wanted to make sure he left on a high note. The chance for Henrik to score was there two or three times that day, but he didn't manage to add to the fifteen goals that he had scored against Rangers in his seven seasons with Celtic. I also had a chance to score when he set me up, but I missed from a few yards out.

David Marshall had a couple of good saves for us, and Stefan Klos had a few good stops for them. Rangers also had Frank de Boer playing for them, and he was superb at the back. I didn't really appreciate what an outstanding footballer he was until I played against him a couple of times. I have a lot of respect for him and his twin brother. However, the Rangers rearguard never find it easy coping with the long ball, and we scored in injury time thanks to that tactic. Marshall's clearance was flicked on by Sutton for Larsson, who found Sutty with the return ball. Chris then spotted Klos off his line and chipped a lovely right-foot effort over the keeper and into the net. It was a wonderful finish.

I know we're criticised for playing the long ball sometimes, but it has given us so much over the years, and we've won countless points from Rangers by using that strategy. The simple truth is that if Rangers – or any other side – struggle to cope with Sutton and Hartson in the air then we try to take advantage of that. There's no shame in playing to your strengths, but I also think we play excellent football and wouldn't have won three titles and reached the final of a European tournament if we had no idea how to get the ball down, take a touch and make a pass. It's insulting to call us nothing but a long-ball side, but the medals and trophies make up for the criticism from certain quarters.

I know Henrik would have loved to have netted that day, but he was just as happy to see Chris get the winner. They had become very good friends at Celtic and enjoyed a great relationship on and off the pitch. At least Henrik departed with another league medal and Scottish Cup medal in his pocket.

It was always going to be difficult to beat Rangers without him but we went into the first Old Firm game of the 2004–05 season determined to show that we were capable. We were in a good mood going into the match as we were already two points ahead of them in the league and had just signed Juninho, who was brave enough to take Henrik's No. 7 squad number. Rangers were maybe not as positive as they might have been, as they had just been knocked out of the Champions League qualifier against CSKA Moscow. I can't remember an Old Firm game where we had so much possession but created as few clear chances. Rangers had plenty of new faces in their team, and it was obvious that Alex McLeish had made it a priority to sign big, powerful guys to stop us being as dominant at set-pieces. They had Jean-Alain Boumsong, Grégory Vignal, Dado Prso and Dragan Mladenovic in their starting line-up and it did give their side a more physical appearance. They also had big Marvin Andrews on the bench.

That afternoon, Rangers defended well and it took a wonder goal from Alan Thompson to give us the points. Late in the game, he struck a powerful left-foot shot from just outside the box, and it bulleted its way high into the net beyond Klos. It put us five points ahead of Rangers, and we were delighted. It was also our seventh straight victory against our oldest rivals, which made our win all the sweeter.

I was also pleased to see Juninho have a fine debut and was happy that he was given a standing ovation when he was substituted for Joos Valgaeren with a couple of minutes left in the match. He's a really nice guy, and Paulina and I socialised with him and his wife a few times when he was with the club. However, after that game, when he displayed exceptional skills and movement, things didn't quite go his way, and he left halfway through the season. I got quite close to the little Brazilian and we spent a lot of time in each other's company. He was disappointed that things didn't work out for him at Celtic but had no regrets about joining the club. He is a great professional and a great footballer. Celtic should always be looking to recruit players of his class.

Juninho started the next Old Firm game at Ibrox in the quarter-final of the CIS Cup on 10 November. I went into that tie short of 100 per cent fitness, having picked up a nasty shoulder injury against Shakhtar Donetsk the week before. I shouldn't have played but was strapped up and had to go out and give my best for the team.

It was a typical ding-dong battle, and we took the lead with yet another goal by John Hartson. He did well to shake off Marvin Andrews and managed to get his head on the end of an Alan Thompson corner to score. We thought we had it sewn up, but they hit back with just six minutes to go when Prso scored with a tap-in. I was absolutely shattered, and I was in pain with my injury. The manager took me off, and Craig Beattie came on in my place. In the first period of extra time, Rangers scored the winning goal when they hit us on the counter-attack, Shota Arveladze finishing off a move with a fine, low strike past David Marshall from the edge of the box. We were all gutted as we were convinced that we could and should have held out after taking the lead.

Our only consolation was the fact we were due to face Rangers again just ten days later in the league. Well, at least we thought it was a good thing, but it turned out to be a nightmare. It was the lowest that I had felt at Ibrox since my debut there. We lost 2–0 in what was a horrible game of football to play in. I absolutely detested that 90 minutes. There was a nasty atmosphere on the pitch, and, on a few occasions, I thought some players were not too far from losing it. I am surprised no one ended up by having a full-scale fight. We had Alan Thompson and Chris Sutton sent off, and Rangers were fortunate not to have any players red-carded by referee Kenny Clark. I didn't get myself involved in any of the off the ball stuff as it's just not my style. I hate to see players squaring up to each other and fighting. It doesn't do anyone any good. In my opinion, the reason we were so successful under Martin O'Neill was that we concentrated on playing football. Of course, we were a powerful side and used the strength of our players to help us win, but after Thommo's red card for squaring up to Peter Lovenkrands, we forgot about playing football. I was angry at the reaction of the Rangers winger. He took it way too far, and I'd like to think, in hindsight, that he feels embarrassed about it.

Nacho Novo scored from the penalty spot, and a header from Prso gave Rangers their two-goal victory. Sutton was sent off on the 55-minute mark for his second yellow, and from then on it was all about holding on and keeping the score as respectable as possible. After the game, with the use of video evidence, Henri Camara and Nacho Novo were given retrospective red cards, and it was hard to disagree with either punishment.

The game dominated the football headlines for days afterwards, and we thought we'd have to wait until 20 February the following year to face Rangers again. However, the Scottish Cup draw threw us together again, this time at Parkhead. There was genuine concern from different people around the country – including Scottish First Minister Jack McConnell – that a repeat of the last Old Firm nonsense might take place, and there was an effort from everyone to make sure that the headlines after the game would be about football and nothing else.

I was still reeling from the blows left by the last two defeats to Rangers, and I was determined not to be a part of a Celtic team that lost three on the trot to them. There was a great atmosphere in training as we prepared for the game, and, I have to say, I was also pleased that Rangers sold Boumsong in the build-up. The ins and outs of it don't concern me, but purely from my perspective as a footballer, I thought it was great news for Celtic. Boumsong is a quality defender and played really well against us in the two victories earlier that season. I'm not saying that he won the games on his own, but he did make a major contribution, and we were happy to see the back of him.

You Can Call Me Stan

O'Neill decided to go with the strike pairing of Chris Sutton and John Hartson, and it worked an absolute treat as they terrorised the Rangers central defensive partnership of Zurab Khizanishvili and Marvin Andrews. Once again, we scored from a long ball. How many times have we punished Rangers in the past five seasons for their inability to handle us in the air? Klos kept Rangers in the game with a string of good saves but had no answer on the 36-minute mark when Khizanishvili couldn't get the better of big John from a clearance from Rab Douglas. Sutton knew what was coming and was on to the knock-down before Andrews had reacted. Chris kept his composure to slide the ball through Klos from about 12 yards out. We were quite comfortable for the rest of the half but knew we couldn't go to sleep or we'd be punished.

Fernando Ricksen equalized for Rangers just two minutes into the second half, and it gave them and their fans a huge lift. They had a couple of new players in their squad that day – Bojan Djordjic and Thomas Buffel – and must have felt like they had a chance of getting a draw and taking us back to Ibrox for a replay. But we have tremendous belief and feel we can win any game, especially when it is at Celtic Park. We kept going at them and Hartson scored the winner for us on the 77-minute mark. Didier Agathe delivered a low cross from the right into the box, but Chris Sutton couldn't reach it. It bounced towards the back post, and, once again, Andrews didn't react in time, leaving Hartson to knock the ball past Klos from six or seven yards with his left foot.

There was no doubt that we deserved to win, and it was a relief to everyone that the game was incident free. None of the nonsense of the previous game was evident, and Hugh Dallas handled the game well, only producing yellow cards for routine stuff.

Our victory meant that Rangers hadn't beaten us for 11 games at Celtic Park – their last win on our patch was back in March 2000. Also, Alex McLeish had yet to beat us at Parkhead, which was a record that we were fiercely proud of and worked hard to maintain. Unfortunately, it was a record that couldn't last much longer, and

McLeish finally ended the run when Rangers beat us 2–0 in a league game on 20 February 2005.

We didn't play well but they scored with soft goals. Vignal grabbed the first on 70 minutes when big Rab should have saved his shot from 25 yards. Sadly, he didn't get his body behind it, and it was a sore one for him. Rab had to suffer days and days of headlines in the newspapers about his mistake, and I felt some of it was over the top. He is now away to Leicester City, and I wish him all the best there. Nacho Novo – my neighbour in Glasgow's West End – scored Rangers' second, and the league was blown wide open.

Craig Bellamy made his debut for us in that game and had a chance to put us ahead in the first half but shot straight at the keeper. I think he was surprised at the ferocity of the fixture and knew he was desperate to make amends the next time we faced Rangers. His chance came on 24 April in the sixth Old Firm meeting of the season. It was the first after the SPL split and victory that day would put us five points ahead with just four games to go. Bellamy got the goal he craved, and I also netted with a header as we won 2–1. My opener came on 21 minutes when I got on the end of a Didier Agathe cross to head home from about 14 yards out. I was overjoyed with that goal and probably went a little over the top as I celebrated in front of the Rangers fans. For my trouble, someone threw a paper cup full of Coke, and it caught me full on. Bellamy scored an excellent goal to put us further ahead before half-time. Rangers then grabbed a lifeline late in the game through Stevie Thompson, but we held on to take full points.

We thought we had taken a major step towards the title at that point – and so did Rangers – but we lost our next match to Hibs, and that cut the gap to two points. Going into the final game of the season we were still two points ahead of our rivals, but they had better goal difference. All we had to do was beat Motherwell at Fir Park. Rangers were facing Hibs at Easter Road, but it shouldn't have mattered to us what they did that afternoon.

We woke up on the Sunday of the match to newspaper headlines declaring that Martin O'Neill was leaving and Gordon Strachan was set to take over as manager of the club. However, nothing was confirmed to us before the game. Everyone was concentrating on beating Motherwell to win our fourth title in five years under the gaffer. Naturally, we were confident we were going to do it.

Sutty put us in front, and we should have been on our way. Later in the match, with the score still at 1–0, we heard that Rangers were also winning. When it got to the last five minutes of the game, Motherwell were really coming at us. We were knackered, playing deeper and deeper in our own half, right on top of big Rab. I could sense the disaster that was coming. We had been unable to keep clean sheets in too many games that season, and the inevitable happened when Scott McDonald scored twice in the last three minutes to give Motherwell the win and hand Rangers the title.

There was nobody to blame apart from ourselves. We should have had the game won after about an hour but missed a couple of chances, and our former keeper Gordon Marshall made a few good saves. Our lack of concentration cost us dearly. We switched off and lost goals. It was a familiar story that season.

There was silence in the dressing-room for about 45 minutes after the final whistle. We couldn't believe it; we were numb. All we could think about was how we had managed to lose the title rather than Rangers winning it. The gaffer came in and didn't say anything. There was nothing to be said. No words or actions were going to change things or make anything better. He just sat in a corner of the dressing-room, took his specs off and put his head in his hands. I felt sorry for him. It shouldn't have ended that way for him. He deserved to leave Celtic with another title on his CV. His demeanour was so different from the way it had been after we had beaten Rangers 2–1 at Ibrox just a few weeks earlier. I can't recall ever having seen him happier in the dressing-room after a game. He was going around kissing all the players!

On the bus back to Parkhead from Fir Park, a few of the players were chatting. It's all a bit of a blur: I can only really remember Lenny and Sutty saying that we didn't deserve to lose the title like that. By then, we sensed that the manager was leaving Celtic to look after his wife Geraldine, who had been battling cancer for over a year. Speculation in the media that O'Neill was quitting and Strachan was taking over had been non-stop.

The players were called to a meeting the next Wednesday morning, three days after we had lost to Motherwell and just three days before we were due to play Dundee United in the Tennent's Scottish Cup final. I was hoping that Martin was going to say that his wife was recovering well and that he was going to be able to stay on as manager. Despite the fact that he'd delivered some incredible speeches in the dressing-room – and I've also heard him being extremely funny doing after-dinner stuff – he came across as perhaps being a little bit nervous. We were all sitting down, and he just said, 'Well, that's it. Lads, I'm leaving.' He told us a new manager would be coming in, and it would be a chance for the players who hadn't been featuring under him to prove him wrong and be a success with Celtic. He thanked all the personnel for their efforts and wished us all the best in the future.

Robbo started to say a few words, but it was all very emotional by that stage, and the occasion got too much for him. He started to cry, and his tears were shared by a few of us. I was sorry to see them leaving. Martin O'Neill had given me the freedom of the pitch and the chance to be myself. Under his leadership I had started to enjoy my football again and enjoy what being a Celtic player should be all about.

As I sat there, memories flashed through my mind. I thought about the great European nights we had: beating Juventus and Barcelona, and the whole Seville experience. Would we ever see the like again?

Gordon Strachan is now the manager and has a hard act to follow, but he was a winner as a player and had a successful career, spanning more than 20 years. He has a fine track record as a manager, and I'm sure he will prove to be an excellent appointment.

9

Seville

The spacious dressing-rooms inside the Gottlieb Daimler Stadium are possibly the most impressive that I've ever been in. I remember sitting in the huge bath after our UEFA Cup tie against Stuttgart, chatting to Neil Lennon. We had just lost 3–2 in the fourth round but were into the quarter-final 5–4 on aggregate. All the lads were physically and mentally shattered at the final whistle, and it was nice to lie back and relax in the hot, soapy water.

Lenny had my full attention as we sat and talked about different points from the game. He told me that he genuinely believed that we could go all the way and win the tournament. I can't deny that at the start of every season I have a little dream that we can win every tournament we enter, but it is next to impossible to do so. It was hard for me to envisage Celtic winning a European tournament, considering that the club had struggled to get past the third round of any of the Continent's competitions for the previous 20 years.

However, sitting in that bath in Stuttgart it was difficult to disagree with Neil because I actually believed him and felt the same way. I really felt we could win the UEFA Cup.

You Can Call Me Stan

There was something about the group of players at the club at that time that made me believe there was no club going to stand in the way of us creating our own piece of European history. We had great players who were growing in confidence with every passing 90 minutes and capable of winning games against any opposition. We really felt like we wouldn't lose any games.

We ended up coming so close to winning the UEFA Cup, and only a goal in extra time by Porto prevented us from doing so. We lost 3–2 on that warm, sunny evening in Seville, and I was inconsolable. We all were. In fact, losing to Porto haunts me to this day. I still have moments when the game flashes through my mind, and I start to think how good it would have been to receive a medal for winning the tournament. I have serious doubts that I will ever come as close to winning a competition like it again, and not winning that final will be a regret that I will carry with me for the rest of my life.

It was a roller-coaster ride to Seville. We were given virtually no chance in a lot of the games but defied the odds time and time again to deliver the goods. We had to work very, very hard to win some of those ties, and we overcame some disgusting behaviour on and off the pitch from some of the teams we faced along the way. We were slaughtered by the likes of Blackburn manager Graeme Souness and his skipper Garry Flitcroft. Everyone at Celtic, from Martin O'Neill down, took so much enjoyment from knocking them out.

We played Rovers in the second round, but before we met them, we had to play FK Suduva from Lithuania. We went into the tie still depressed from losing to FC Basel in the Champions League qualifier a few weeks earlier. With all due respect to Suduva, they were just the kind of opposition that we needed to play against in Europe at that time. We knew we would win the tie easily, and it was a chance to score a few goals and get rid of our Champions League hangover.

We played the Lithuanians at home in the first leg and won 8–1. Henrik Larsson scored a hat-trick that night to equal Ally

McCoist's record of 21 goals scored in European competition with a Scottish club. I scored our third with a volley from the edge of the box, and I was delighted with the strike. Chris Sutton, Paul Lambert, John Hartson and Joos Valgaeren scored our other goals. We were sloppy towards the end, allowing Suduva to score an injury-time goal courtesy of Tomas Radzinevicius.

The second leg was a formality, and with an Old Firm game just around the corner, the gaffer decided to rest a few players. Neil Lennon, Chris Sutton, Bobo Balde and Henrik Larsson were all excluded from the travelling party. David Fernandez and Alan Thompson scored our goals to give us a 2–0 victory, and we went through 10–1 on aggregate.

The draw for the next round was made on the Friday, and we were excited – as always – to see who we would meet. My preference would be for an easy tie every time, but we came out of the glass bowl with Blackburn, and straight away it was tagged the 'Battle of Britain'.

I could sense the likes of Sutton, Thompson and Lennon were really up for the tie. They had played in England for many years, and to come up to Scotland to ply their trade had not been regarded as a good move by many down south. Some people don't give Scottish football the respect it deserves.

Graeme Souness was trying to play the fixture down, and his comments before the first leg at Celtic Park were along the lines that he didn't care about beating us, he was only interested in avoiding relegation from the Premiership. Of course, the fact that he was a former manager of Rangers and had taken great delight in beating Celtic when he had first come to Scotland to take over the Ibrox club in 1986 meant there was added spice. The Celtic fans wanted to beat him more than anything else, and he wanted to beat Celtic more than anything else – that's for sure.

Souness made a point of going out on to the track to applaud the Blackburn travelling support and then walked back to the technical area with a huge smile on his face. He was trying to wind up our supporters, but it didn't work. I wasn't very impressed with him, and I was just as happy as the English guys at our club that we managed to knock them out.

Blackburn went into the game full of confidence and with a strike partnership of Dwight Yorke and Andy Cole – a pair that combined so well to help Manchester United win the Champions League in 1999 – a quality wide player in Damien Duff and goalkeeper Brad Friedel in the form of his life, they were right to believe they could knock us out.

We didn't play anywhere near the level we knew we were capable of in the first half and allowed them too much time and room on the ball. Yet we could have been ahead by the break had Friedel not denied me a goal by pulling off a fantastic save from a header. The manager had words with us at half-time and told us to have more belief and take the game to them. We were pumped up after that and never looked back. We gradually took control, and Henrik scored the winner for us with just six minutes left.

John Hartson came on as a sub for Paul Lambert on 75 minutes, and he played his part in the winner when he got up to head Alan Thompson's corner towards goal. It looked a cert, but Friedel blocked it on the line. Thankfully, the ball broke loose and fell to Larsson, who made no mistake.

Henrik had broken McCoist's record and had also rammed the pre-match comments by Souness down the Blackburn gaffer's throat. Before the match he had claimed that Henrik still had to prove himself at the top level. I was glad Souness was made to eat his words after the first leg, and he should have learned his lesson, but he obviously can't stop himself from making derogatory comments. He was at it again right after the final whistle when he claimed his side were much better than us and that it was 'men against boys' on the Parkhead pitch that night. Blackburn skipper Garry Flitcroft also took a pop at us. Talk about trying to wind us up. O'Neill was really angry at the comments made by Souness and so were the players. The second leg couldn't come quickly enough, but, unfortunately, we had to wait two weeks to meet them again.

Our preparation for the return leg was good and we headed

down to Blackburn full of confidence. The manager changed it about a bit for that game and played Hartson and Larsson as his front combination with Sutton in behind them. I dropped back a bit to play alongside Lennon in the centre of midfield. Lambert was on the bench, and it must have been difficult for him to miss out on such a huge game, but he was the ultimate professional that night. He supported the lads, giving us words of encouragement and advice on the day of the game.

It was a wet night, and when we ran out for the start of the game it was heartening to see so many Celtic fans inside the stadium. They gave us great backing that night and totally overshadowed the English fans. In the same way that they dominated the stands, we controlled the game. From start to finish, we outplayed the Premiership side, and we scored the vital away goal in the first half. Henrik netted, and then Sutton scored against his old side on 68 minutes when he made a clever run to the front post to get on the end of my corner kick and head past Friedel. We could have won by four or five that night. Goal scorers are always the guys that matter in the eyes of most people, but, I have to say, I thought Joos Valgaeren and Didier Agathe were tremendous over the two legs. Joos defended so well, and Didier made sure Damien Duff never got the chance to create anything for his teammates. Duff looked nothing like a £20 million player that night. I was so happy for the guys and manager that we won. Souness and his players showed us no respect, and I don't recall ever seeing the gaffer or the likes of Sutton, Thompson and Lennon so happy after a victory. Our manager put Souness in his place. The rest of the lads loved putting one over on him and made the English media and pundits eat their words, after they had given us little chance of winning.

And so we marched on. Our plastic ball was back in the glass bowl for the third-round draw at the UEFA headquarters. We were pulled out of the hat with Celta Vigo. Once again, we were on the receiving end of some disrespectful remarks from the opposition manager going into the game. It was a theme that seemed to run right through our UEFA Cup campaign that season.

You Can Call Me Stan

This time it was Celta's Miguel Ángel Lotina. He said that we were guilty of 'playing football like headless chickens'. Again, we didn't play to the best of our capabilities in the first half of the first leg, and, at that stage, Lotina must have felt that his pre-match comments were absolutely spot on.

Our manager knew differently but had to give us a more than gentle reminder that we were falling short of the standard required to win European games at that level. His half-time words were taken on board. We took the lead on 51 minutes when Henrik scored another European goal. As ever, he was sniffing about the six-yard box and reacted before everyone else to get on the end of a Hartson header across goal from a Steve Guppy corner.

The game finished that way, and we were pleased to have recorded another clean sheet at home. We would also go to northern Spain with a one-goal advantage. Celta Vigo had played well, and there was a doubt in my mind that we would be able to go to their place and get the result we needed. They were a much better side than Blackburn, and I knew we were going to have to put in a real defensive shift in the second leg to do enough to knock them out.

Going into a game in an intimidating venue against a team from a country that is rated in Europe, you always hope for a strong referee. The last thing you want is an official who will cave in. In the first leg we had a French ref by the name of Claude Columbo, and he was inconsistent. He sent our gaffer to the stand with a few minutes of the game remaining and seemed to enjoy dismissing him.

Vigo was a nice city, and the temperature there was much more pleasant than the December weather we left behind in Glasgow. I always look forward to going to different cities, and I like to see different stadiums. I suppose I tried to build up a picture in my mind of what Vigo's ground was going to be like, and I had visions of it being breathtaking. However, it was far from spectacular and was in need of renovation.

In the match, Vigo put us under tremendous pressure from the kick-off and played with a swagger as they passed the ball about. We had to scrap for every ball and keep them out of our final third of the pitch. They had chances, but Bobo Balde made some good tackles, and Rab Douglas pulled off a couple of really good saves.

A Celta goal looked inevitable, and they got one on 22 minutes when a Jesus Mora Nieto Jesuli shot deflected off Ulrik Laursen and flew into the net. Not unusually, our heads went down at that point, and we just had to concentrate on getting through the next few minutes unscathed.

Celta were driven on by their supporters, to the point that there was a nasty atmosphere in the air, and I felt that the game wasn't going to last the 90 minutes without some sort of serious incident. Tackles were flying in all over the pitch, and Claus Bo-Larsen, the Danish referee, booked a few players.

Such was the pressure applied by Vigo and the confidence that they gained after the goal, it was hard to see us surviving an hour without conceding another. Deep down we all knew we'd have to score to stay in the tie. Thankfully, we managed to level on the 36-minute mark. Big John Hartson used his phenomenal upper-body strength to shake off Eduardo Berrizo at the edge of the box, and as he collected a Chris Sutton pass, he created room for himself. He then turned towards goal and unleashed a low shot past José Pinto.

The Vigo players were furious that they didn't receive a free-kick, but the ref was having none of it. That's the kind of thing I meant when I said that you need a strong referee in big games. Peter Luccin then spat on Hartson, but Bo-Larsen missed it. It was a disgusting act: there's no room for that kind of nonsense in football. I was glad that UEFA looked into the incident and banned him after the game.

Vigo took the lead again on 54 minutes. Their goal came about when we were down to ten men due to Lenny receiving treatment for a hamstring pull. They took advantage, and Benni McCarthy grabbed their second. Lambert came on for Lennon and McNamara replaced Hartson. Big John had been on the receiving end of some heavy fouls from the Spanish team. He really played his part that night with his goal and his professionalism – he kept his cool and didn't react to the rough treatment that he received.

For the final twenty minutes – although it felt like three hours – Vigo camped in our half and pounded our goal. Agathe was superb for us: when we gained possession we often just gave him the ball and he would take it for a run down the right wing. In doing so he killed precious seconds, gave the rest of us a chance to catch our breath and allowed the team to regain its composure and shape.

It was agonising stuff, and I reckon there must have been a few fingernails bitten down to the bone by the boys inside our technical area, the supporters in the stands and our fans watching on television back in Scotland. We managed to hang on to win on the away-goals rule to take us beyond Christmas in European football for the first time in 23 years. I was really proud of that achievement. After all the hard work we had put in and the verbal abuse from the opposition that we had to suffer, we deserved to be in the fourth round.

Our next European tie was against Stuttgart in February. I remember that fixture really well. My good friend Krassi Balakov was playing for Stuttgart, and the Bulgarian media were showing a keen interest. Naturally, we both badly wanted to win. However, by the time the first leg came around we were without Henrik, who had picked up a smashed cheekbone in a league game against Livingston. With John Hartson suspended, Shaun Maloney partnered Sutton up front.

When I come up against new opposition, I try to gather as much background information on them as possible. I want to know little things that might help me on the pitch and the team in general. I telephoned my international teammate Marian Hristov to ask him about Stuttgart as he was playing for Kaiserslautern in the Bundesliga at the time. His information was good and helped us to win the tie. He told me that the Stuttgart keeper Timo Hilderbrand was good but sometimes tried to be too clever by trying to anticipate things that the opposition players would do. I stored that away in my head and used it on the 67-minute mark of the first leg to put us 3–1 ahead. Paul Lambert found me with a pass inside the box, and I was about a yard away from the byline on the right wing, approximately eight yards from the keeper's front post.

Now, from that position, ninety-nine times out of one hundred I would have driven the ball low across the six-yard box for one of my teammates, but I knew that Hilderbrand would be expecting that. He was a yard off his line, leaving a narrow gap for the ball to go through. I decided to try my luck and sneaked the ball in at the near post. I suppose some people felt it was a fluke, but because of Marian's information, it was deliberate on my part. I was pleased with the way I played that night. I was also on a real high because our victory came only nine days after young Stiliyan was born.

That third goal gave us a good lead, but we had got off to a bad start. Stuttgart were reduced to ten men after sixteen minutes when Marcelo Bordon was sent off for bringing me down as I ran in on goal. Pierluigi Collina – a top referee – immediately produced the red card. However, Stuttgart showed their quality and took the lead through Kevin Kuranyi. Lambert, who was fantastic for us in the middle of the park, equalized with a great shot. Then, Shaun put us in front with a goal that only good strikers are capable of scoring, managing to get on the end of a defender's poor clearance and, even though he was off balance, somehow squeezing the ball past the keeper.

Having a two-goal advantage meant that we were confident heading over to Germany a week later for the return leg. The Germans came at us right from the first whistle, and we had a couple of close escapes. At that point in the match, I remember thinking that we were going to struggle to get through to the quarter-final. However, Didier came into the game and used his incredible pace to set up two goals for us. His first cross was flicked on by Hartson and was brilliantly converted courtesy of a full-length diving header by Thompson. Didier was up for it that night: a 50-yard run down the wing, later in the match, resulted in a cutback that Sutton banged in.

We were through, although they came back at us to score three times thanks to strikes from Christian Tiffert, Aleksander Hleb and Michael Mutzel. They put us under incredible pressure in the final few minutes but we held on. We lost 3–2 that night but had knocked out an excellent side.

It was around that time that Seville started to get mentioned on a regular basis. I don't think that many people knew where the UEFA Cup final was being played up until then but after we beat Celta that was no longer the case. The Scottish media were right behind our run and the question was now being asked seriously – could we go all the way?

Liverpool were our next opponents; another Battle of Britain loomed. We were given a boost for that game when Henrik declared himself fit, probably about two or three weeks ahead of schedule in the recovery from his jaw injury. We went into the tie believing we could win. Liverpool had top, top players in Steven Gerrard, Michael Owen and Didi Hamann but were not invincible. The atmosphere inside Celtic Park in the minutes up to kick-off was electric. Gerry Marsden belted out 'You'll Never Walk Alone', which was an emotional moment.

With the fans behind us, we were right up for the game and had spoken beforehand about getting at Liverpool early. We wanted to have a typical whirlwind start, instead of a slow, European-style build-up. Within 30 seconds Hartson hit the crossbar. We were all over them. Liverpool were rattled and couldn't put two passes together. Sami Hyypia looked stunned. Then, after just 115 seconds, Henrik scored to give us the perfect start. Hyypia couldn't clear a Hartson cross, and the ball landed at Thompson's feet at the back post. He battered it back across goal and Henrik was there, lurking about, to show off his killer instincts and knock the ball over the line.

We kept going at them and Hartson almost got another. Liverpool, as expected, eventually got going and played some lovely stuff. Emile Heskey equalized, and the game finished level with the outcome firmly in the balance.

There was a disgraceful moment during the game when

Liverpool striker El-Hadji Diouf spat at a Celtic fan. It was a disgusting thing to do and soured a great occasion. Gérard Houllier decided not to play Diouf in the second leg at Anfield, and that was the correct decision. I also suspect that Houllier may well have underestimated us going into the second leg. I think he thought that getting a draw in the first leg was going to be enough for Liverpool to ease through. Well, one thing about us that season was that we had a mentality that meant we never knew when we were beaten. If we did lose, it was because the opposition had produced something really special.

We went to Anfield on the back of losing the CIS League Cup final to Rangers. Chris Sutton picked up an injury in that game and was ruled out for the Liverpool clash. Like the Blackburn tie earlier in the competition we were all wound up for the second Battle of Britain. I suppose that the players who had played down south felt there was yet another point to prove. Winning that tie would demonstrate, beyond any doubt, that we were right up there with the best and more than capable of winning the tournament.

The manager was in excellent form before the game and had us all bursting to go. He not only made us desperate to win for ourselves, he also wanted us to show our detractors that they were wrong to question our abilities. He reminded the guys that there might not be too many nights like that one left for a few of the older guys, and they shouldn't waste the chance to make it one of the greatest nights of their careers. As a result, our dressing-room was really noisy in the seconds leading up to the start of the game. We were all shouting and encouraging each other. We couldn't wait to get out on the pitch.

Johan Mjällby was brilliant that night: he never gave Owen a sniff. Rab Douglas also made one or two good saves. We were solid at the back, and that gave us the platform to get the goals we needed to take us through. Minutes before half-time, Thompson drove home a free-kick through the Liverpool wall from about 22 yards. It was a fabulous strike, and after surviving a few scares in our own area, we scored again to make it 2–0 just nine minutes from the end. Big John played a one–two with Henrik then fired a screamer past Jerzy Dudek from 23 yards out. I was so happy. The scenes of celebration at the end with the fans were more than memorable. We were in the semi-final of a European tournament for the first time in 29 years, and we thoroughly deserved to be there.

The next day we waited for the draw. We were all getting used to sitting by the telly waiting to see who we were going to face. Porto, Lazio and Boavista made up the other semi-finalists, and we were pleased to draw Boavista. They were obviously doing well in Europe but their league form in Portugal was poor. The first leg was to be played at Celtic Park, and I was excited and a little nervous, knowing that there was so much at stake. We were also expected to win the tie, whereas in most, if not all, of the previous rounds, we started as underdogs.

In the first leg, it was 0–0 at half-time, and we hadn't played that well. Boavista were a stuffy, hard-working side with little flair; they shut us down well. The team from Portugal took the lead on 47 minutes when Joos Valgaeren scored an own goal after trying to clear a low cross at the back post from Filipe Anunciação. The silence from our fans was deafening, but they were back on their feet a couple of minutes later when Henrik scored with a shot after I had found him with a nice little pass inside the box. Henrik could have scored again from the spot to give us a lead to take into the second leg in Portugal, but his penalty was saved by their keeper Ricardo.

Henrik was angry with himself, but you know never to write him off. That's why no one was surprised when he scored the goal in the return leg to take us to Seville. It wasn't a great game that night. It was all about doing whatever was needed to score one more than them. Their stadium was in the process of being rebuilt for Euro 2004, and it looked more like a building site. It just wasn't what a venue for the semi-final of a European tournament should have looked like.

Henrik scored the all-important goal with 12 minutes to go in the match. He managed to get a shot in on Ricardo after his intended pass for Hartson rebounded back to him. Ricardo got a hand to Henrik's shot, and it was one of those moments when the ball seems to take an eternity to get over the line. The scenes at the end of the game were wonderful. Players collapsed on the turf, and many of our fans were in tears. It was a great night to be associated with Celtic.

It was a huge win for us, and I was delighted we'd managed to get one over their keeper Ricardo. His time wasting over the two legs was shameful – totally out of order. I'm glad we had the last laugh. Boavista's style, in any shape or form, would not have enhanced the UEFA Cup final.

Porto defeated Lazio, and it meant we would go head to head with another Portuguese side in Seville on 21 May. Everyone had put in so much effort to get to the final. We were still chasing the league, and between that and the European run, the players were giving every last ounce of energy and effort. For the final three months of the season, every time we travelled back from an away match our bus resembled a hospital ward. So many players were carrying injuries but managed to play through the pain barrier. We were all desperate to be involved and nothing – even injury – was going to stand in our way. Sadly, one injury did take its toll: John Hartson wasn't available for the final. He injured his back a few weeks before the big match, and I felt so sorry for him. He had played such a big part in getting us there and didn't deserve to be watching the game from the stand.

The 26 days building up to Seville were crazy. The attention on us was incredible. There wasn't a moment of privacy to be had. We were still chasing the league title but couldn't keep Seville out of our heads. Still, playing big games is what you want as a footballer. I wish I was lucky enough to have that kind of season every year.

My mother, father and brother were at the final. Paulina's mother was also there as were Paulina and young Stiliyan. I also had four friends over from Bulgaria. I was surprised only four of them came because a few more had indicated their desire to travel.

You Can Call Me Stan

I had sorted out hotel accommodation for them because I wanted to make sure they really enjoyed it and had a memorable few days in Spain. But four or five pulled out at the last minute and that disappointed me. It's at times like that that you find out who your true friends are.

I must have given away about 45 or 50 tickets and could have been doing with 200 more. Everyone seemed to want one; even people I met in the street were asking me. There was talk that Celtic fans were paying around £5,000 for a ticket. Money was no object at that time for our supporters, or so it appeared. Indeed, a guy I met on a flight down to London in the weeks leading up to the final asked me to name my price for a ticket. I couldn't get the guy a ticket, and if I could, I would never have taken his money from him.

In the couple of days leading up to the game, we didn't go over the top with our preparations. We watched Porto on video, and the manager pointed out their strengths and weaknesses. Also, because of the heat in Spain, training in the build-up to the game was uncomfortable, and we didn't want to overdo it. We were ready for the game and just wanted it to start. To help relax the players, the manager and backroom staff put on a quiz night before every European game. It was a routine that they stuck with throughout the campaign because it seemed to bring us a bit of luck.

When Stan Varga arrived in the January transfer window he became my room-mate, and I shared with him when we travelled to play Liverpool and Boavista. Stan couldn't play in the European matches because he wasn't registered in time but reckoned he was my lucky charm. I slept well the night before the game, but kept getting up to drink water. Big Stan was brilliant with me, and any time I got up he'd ask if I was OK or if I needed anything. I was just thirsty.

On the afternoon of the game, I tried to take a nap in my room, but I couldn't sleep. I wanted to close my eyes for an hour or so but couldn't close them for a second – I was too excited and nervous. Big Stan was also nervous, and he wasn't even playing!

On the way to the game, our bus got lost. We had a police escort but took a longer route to attempt to avoid the heavy traffic in the city. However, we ended up taking a wrong turn somewhere. We weren't too happy about it and thought 'Why does this have to happen to us, on the night of the biggest game of our lives?'

The manager's team-talk was short and to the point. As we sat in the dressing-room he named the team and said to us, 'Boys, this may well be the biggest game you will ever play in. We've been through all our preparation, you know what you have to do and you know what to expect from Porto. Every player in this dressing-room wants to win this game, and I want you all to go out there and show exactly why you are here.'

Well, we did show exactly why we deserved to be in the final in the beautiful Estadio Olímpico, but it wasn't enough to get us the win we wanted. We were all desperately disappointed to lose. On a personal level, I was very unhappy with my own performance. Part of the problem was that I found it really hard to breathe in the searing heat. It was about 85 degrees Fahrenheit, and I couldn't handle it. I was struggling after about 20 minutes, and I think most of our boys had problems adapting to the sweltering conditions. I felt as though I didn't have enough power in my legs to get about the pitch the way that I wanted and that the game was just passing me by.

My game is all about energy, getting from one penalty box to the other, and it was so frustrating that I wasn't able to perform to that level in one of the biggest games of my life. I always seemed to be in the wrong position, and the ball didn't come my way. I didn't get a break of the ball or one bit of luck all night. For days leading up to the final, I thought about playing well and proving that I had the necessary quality to play at the highest level, but it wasn't to be. It was a major disappointment not to have stamped my authority on the game. I felt like I had played well in all the rounds up to the final and then I let myself, the club and our supporters down on the biggest night of all.

Maybe if we had scored first, or been in the lead at one point, the outcome might have been different. It would have been interesting to see how Porto would have reacted if they had been made to come from behind. But they were in control for long spells and took the lead through Derlei. It was a sloppy goal to concede, and it was sickening to lose one so close to half-time.

Tackles had been flying in throughout the first half, and there were one or two nasty incidents. There was also a bit of a flare-up as we left the pitch at half-time, and it carried on up the tunnel. I didn't see anything but remember the manager urging us during the break to concentrate on playing football and not to get involved in any of the off the ball stuff. He said to us, as he often did, 'We have a better chance of winning the game with 11 men on the pitch.'

We kept our discipline at the start of the second half and ended up equalizing thanks to a goal from Henrik, our prolific striker scoring with a terrific header from a Didier Agathe cross. Unfortunately, we never really got the chance to capitalize on Henrik's goal or gain any impetus from it because Porto were back in the lead when Dimitri Alenitchev scored.

In those situations, the team always looked to Henrik to get us out of a hole, and he came up with the goods again with a quite brilliant header from an Alan Thompson corner to make it 2–2. Honestly, Henrik's technique for that goal – the timing of his jump and the power and accuracy of the header – was phenomenal. He didn't deserve to be on the losing side that night. In my opinion, it was his greatest ever game in a Celtic jersey.

The match went into extra time, but we were severely handicapped after Bobo was sent off for his second bookable offence. The heat was hard enough to cope with, but playing against them with a man down was always likely to be too much. Of course, Porto had no such problems with the heat. They came from a warm climate, and it was just another night at the office for them. They eventually scored the winner on the 114-minute mark when Derlei scored from the edge of the box. Sadly, there was no way back for us.

I was subbed in the second period of extra time and was surprised to be taken off. Despite not playing well, I always felt I could have scored or set one up. When I was walking off I was really down because I knew my final was over and there was nothing more I could do to help us get back into the game. I was sad but put a brave face on it. I sat in the technical area with the rest of the boys and cheered us on, praying we would score another goal. It was the manager's decision to sub me, and I respected it. He sees the bigger picture and made the decision because he thought it would help us to avoid defeat. His only thoughts were of getting us the goal we needed to take his team into a penalty shoot-out. I came off for young Shaun Maloney, and he played fine but couldn't grab us the goal that would have levelled the match.

Porto wasted a lot of time in the closing minutes, and it was incredibly frustrating for us. However, if we had been in the same position, we might have done the same. Let's be honest, we would have wasted time – not getting the ball back quickly enough, celebrating for longer than normal when we scored a goal. It's not the sporting thing to do, and it was very frustrating when we were trying to equalize, but it happens in football. I'd never pat the Porto players on the back for doing it, but I don't really want to criticise them either because time wasting goes on in football – it always has and always will.

Right after the game, the manager told us that we should be proud of ourselves and that some of us might be back in a similar position again. We had to forget about the loss and concentrate on going to Kilmarnock for our next match, which we had to win to give us a chance of clinching the league title. Of course, we eventually lost the league to Rangers by one goal. The season, after promising so much, ended trophyless.

I still have my runner-up medal from the UEFA Cup final. I keep it in my house. I know some footballers don't want to accept second best, and I'm also like that, but I'd never be the type to throw away a medal. It would have been better to have lifted the medal that the Porto players walked away with but that didn't happen, and there is nothing anyone can do to change the outcome of the game.

I've watched the game three times since, but it doesn't get any easier to take in and accept. However, that medal from Seville brings back a lot of happy memories: memories of how we got there and some of the glorious nights along the way. I will never forget the highs that we experienced in reaching the 2003 UEFA Cup final.

10

European Adventures

The celebrations after our league win in 2001 were fantastic, but it was the realisation afterwards of what was still to come that made it even more special – we had qualified for the Champions League. I had watched UEFA's premier competition on TV, dreaming that I'd one day get the chance to play in it. Now here I was, only 180 minutes of football against Ajax away from making my ambition a reality.

The roller-coaster ride we had to go through during the next three months was unbelievable – from dodgy penalties to the ultimate heartbreak – but it was all worth it. Getting there was never going to be easy, though. Ajax weren't the team they used to be but were still a formidable force, and we knew it was going to take two special performances to get us through to the 'Promised Land' of the Champions League.

I travelled to Holland for the first leg despite the fact that I was nowhere near fit after my leg break. I was grateful to Martin O'Neill for inviting me and making me feel part of it. It was a great experience to sit in the Amsterdam ArenA and watch us win 3–1.

You Can Call Me Stan

The look on the faces of the Ajax officials and their fans that night was priceless. We caught the Dutch champions cold – they obviously thought it would be a formality to beat us and reach the group stages.

Everything just seemed to click that night. Bobby Petta and Didier Agathe were superb out wide, and Jackie McNamara was fantastic in the centre of midfield. I remember jumping to my feet when our goals from Bobby, Didier and Chris Sutton hit the net – I felt so proud. I wanted to run onto the pitch to hug them and join in the celebrations because I knew that performance had more or less guaranteed us a place in the Champions League.

The second leg was all about protecting our lead and making sure that we didn't lose on aggregate. Ajax came at us with the ferocity of a team with nothing to lose, but we coped well with the pressure, although there were spells in the game when they did give us the run around. However, that night wasn't about silky football and going for broke – it was about maintaining our precious 3–1 advantage. The fact that we lost 1–0 at home was disappointing, but the most important thing was that we were through.

I was in the squad for the return leg because I had just about regained my fitness, but I had to settle for a seat in the stand again. Despite not playing, my guts were churning during the match because so much was at stake, and the relief I felt when the referee blew for time-up was incredible. It was one of the best feelings I have ever experienced in football and that tells you how much it meant to me because I wasn't even playing. I ran down to the dressing-room after the game to congratulate the boys, and the place was jumping. I just remember Didier coming over and asking me, 'How happy are you now that we've made it?' That brought it home to me.

Most of us were Champions League rookies so we were going to relish it and make the most of every single moment. I think the likes of Henrik Larsson, Tom Boyd, Jackie McNamara and Paul Lambert felt it even more than most of us because they had been through the agony of not making it to the group stages when Jozef Vengloš was the manager in 1998.

I was pretty happy with our first Champions League draw – Juventus, Porto and Rosenborg. It gave us a decent chance of going through to the next stage. Our first game was supposed to be on 12 September against Rosenborg at home, and we were at our hotel just getting ready for a light morning training session when we heard that UEFA had cancelled all games that night as a mark of respect for the thousands who had lost their lives in the terrorist bombings in New York and Washington the day before. I didn't know anyone involved in the atrocities but still felt a sense of loss; I think most people did.

The previous day, in our hotel on the outskirts of Glasgow, I had watched the aftermath of the World Trade Center attack unfold. It was horrible to sit and watch those scenes on television. The images left me numb – it was like something out of a movie – and the gravity of the situation took a while to sink in. All the players and management felt so sorry for the people who had lost their lives that day and for the family and friends that they left behind in such tragic circumstances.

That night, the gaffer warned us that our game against Rosenborg could be called off, but we still had to prepare properly. The game was of course postponed, and I think UEFA made the correct decision. Yes, it was an anti-climax for us – we were ready to play in front of 60,000 of our fans at Parkhead in the club's first ever Champions League game and all of a sudden it was taken away – but, really, we had no complaints. It wasn't a time to moan about a bit of disruption to a few football games.

As a result of the postponement of the Rosenborg match, it meant that our opening Champions League game would be against Juventus in Turin. Nice easy start, eh? I suspect 90 per cent of football people expected us to lose. And lose heavily. After all, this was Celtic against *Juventus* – a team coached by Marcello Lippi with superstars like Lilian Thuram, Alessandro Del Piero, Pavel Nedved, David Trezeguet and Marcelo Salas in their team.

You Can Call Me Stan

Lippi had spent around £90 million during the summer on new players. Martin O'Neill had spent around £6 million on Bobo Balde, John Hartson, Momo Sylla and Steve Guppy. But football isn't played on paper – it doesn't always work out the way you think when it comes to the real thing.

I remember packing my bags for the flight on the Monday morning into Turin, and I felt so positive. I had just netted against Dundee on the Saturday night in a 4–0 league win, and it was one of the best goals I've ever scored. We were leading 2–0 at the time and had a free-kick about 35 yards out. Normally Henrik, Lubo Moravcik or Alan Thompson would have a go, but Henrik asked me if I fancied a strike. I like taking free-kicks and jumped at the chance. When Henrik tapped the ball to the side for me I just struck it as hard as I could. I was delighted when it hit the net and not just because it was a spectacular goal. It was also my first since returning from my broken leg, and that meant so much to me. My recovery took a giant step forward that night.

For away matches in Europe the manager gives the players the option of travelling on the team bus from Parkhead or making our own way to the airport. Most of the time, I go my own way and leave the car at the airport. On the day that the team were due to leave for Italy, Paulina was just as excited as me about the Champions League and was up at 6 a.m. You would have thought she was going to play beside me in the middle of the park! She drove me to the airport, and when we arrived the photographers and journalists were all waiting for us. They wanted a bit of everyone, and that kind of attention, once again, hammered home just what the tournament meant to everyone and the importance of it across Europe.

When we stepped off the plane it was the Italian media's turn to hound us round the airport. They wanted to know everything, and I don't think there's such a thing as a quick interview with them. Microphone after microphone was thrust into my face whether I liked it or not. But I felt like a million dollars. We had our club suits on, and I was so proud to be wearing the uniform of Celtic, preparing to play in the Champions League for my team against a side that had won the trophy twice.

We stayed at a lovely hotel in Milan, and I shared with Colin Healy, who was to be my room-mate for the entire Champions League campaign. He's a really nice guy, and we had some good fun together. I wished him well when he went to Sunderland, but I was absolutely gutted for him when he broke his leg twice in his first 14 months down there. Colin didn't deserve that bad luck. We keep in regular contact, and I know he'll recover and go on to have a good career at club and international level with Ireland.

I enjoy having a room-mate, but some of the boys prefer to be on their own in case the other guy snores or wants to sit up all night watching TV! All the players are different when it comes to relaxing on away trips. Some like to play cards, while some like to have a cup of coffee or a Coke and a chat. Others like Henrik, Jackie and Paul Lambert like to play golf on the PlayStation. On the Milan trip, I just wanted an early night to give me a good sleep to prepare for the big day ahead.

We had an excellent meal, and I had my usual spaghetti bolognese. We were in Italy, and, fittingly, it was the finest spag bol I had ever tasted. After dinner we usually like to go out for a walk, providing that the weather is decent. It gives us the chance to enjoy a change of scenery and an opportunity to have a blether. Going out for a stroll also gives the boys a chance to see a small part of the country that we are visiting. It's always nice to take back a small memory of the place in which we're playing.

That night, Paul Lambert played a real captain's role and spent a couple of minutes with a few players going over what to expect in the Champions League. He tried to drum it into us that no one should be nervous and that we should just enjoy every minute of the experience.

The build-up to the game was incredible. There is such an amazing atmosphere associated with the Champions League. I had only watched it on television and it always looked spectacular, the kind of stage you dream about playing on. However, despite all the brouhaha, our build-up was spot on and we were all really relaxed. The manager was calm and his team-talk was to the point: we all knew what he wanted us to do. I liked the manager's team-talks because they were never long and complicated. He always kept them sharp and to the point – every word meant something. He didn't go on and on for the sake of it.

Despite the positive team-talk, we found ourselves two goals down against Juve, and, to be honest, it must have looked as though we were going to lose by five or six. But not long into the second half we started getting it together and had the Italians a little worried. We won a free-kick about 30 yards out, and I was itching to take it after my goal against Dundee a few days earlier. Then again, I wasn't sure about asking to take it because I didn't want to cause any arguments on the pitch if any of the others fancied it. However, Henrik came up to me and said, 'How about it?' He didn't have to ask twice. He rolled the ball to me, and I struck it as hard as I could. I didn't even know I had scored because there were too many bodies in front of me. I could see a couple of the boys throw their arms in the air, but I still wasn't sure where my shot had landed. I looked to the referee, and when he pointed back to the centre circle I knew it was in. I was overjoyed to score such an important goal against Juventus in their own back yard, and to be the first Celtic player to score in the Champions League group stages was also special.

When I scored I didn't go too mad because the players just wanted to get on with the game to try and grab an equalizer. We felt the opportunity was there for us to get another goal and come away with a point. It looked as though it might happen when Edgar Davids was sent off, and the Juventus players started to argue amongst themselves, which is always a good sign. Minutes later, we were awarded a penalty when Sutton was fouled. Henrik was as cool as you like and put the ball past Gigi Buffon to bring us level. But the drama wasn't over. A few minutes later, the German referee Helmut Krug awarded them a penalty when Nicola Amoruso collapsed inside the box after Joos Valgaeren 'challenged' him. Joos hardly touched him, and I couldn't believe it when the ref gave them a penalty. Amoruso scored to give Juve a last-minute winner. It just wasn't right – we didn't deserve to have the points snatched away from us with a decision as bad as that. In the end, that single point cost us our place in the next stage, and I hope we never come across Mr Krug again. We'll certainly be ready for him if he shows up anywhere near a Celtic game again. One of the boys mentioned that a dark alley would probably be the preferred location to bump into him, though!

I walked off the pitch in disgust and didn't even think about exchanging a jersey with a Juventus player as is the norm after European games. I think even they were embarrassed about the referee's decision, although some of them had the cheek to say that Krug had got it right. Unbelievable.

The dressing-room was as quiet as I have ever heard it under Martin O'Neill. The players couldn't believe it, but, more importantly, we had to console Joos and tell him that it wasn't his fault. The manager was raging with the penalty decision and must have been worried about what long-term damage it could do to the team psychologically. He was sent to the stand that night for questioning the penalty call and had plenty on his mind worrying about what suspension UEFA would impose on him for his behaviour. He was an angry man and had every right to be.

Martin made his way round every player and told us that we should be proud of our performance. He said that it was only bad luck – not our display – that had prevented us from taking at least a point back to Glasgow. Nevertheless, the journey home was miserable. From the moment the final whistle blew till the moment I got back to my house took about six hours, and not a minute of it went by without the game going round and round in my head. The plane journey was a quiet one – I think everybody just wanted to get home and feel like it was over.

Thankfully, we didn't let it spill over into our domestic form and a few days later we beat Aberdeen 2–0 in the league at home, and I scored from another free-kick – my third in a row. I don't like to boast but just for the record, although I didn't score in our next game – against Porto – I did get a goal in the game after that against Rangers. It was another free-kick as well. Four goals in five games – all from similar areas of the pitch. To finish off a rewarding month, I picked up the Bank of Scotland Player of the Month award for September. It's always nice to be recognised and appreciated by other people involved in the game.

The next Champions League match was at home to Porto, and although it was only our second, we knew we had to win it. It was a nervous 90 minutes, and the Portuguese side had a couple of chances, but we managed to get the three points thanks to Larsson's first-half goal. Henrik is world class. The way he came back from his leg break to net 53 goals the next season and win Europe's Golden Boot was a tremendous achievement. I know what it's like to come back from such an injury, and believe me, it's not easy.

I am still coming to terms with life without Henrik at Celtic. Before he eventually left last summer to join Barcelona, I was so happy that he had knocked back the chance to move to another club in Europe. I believe that he would have had several attractive options had he made it known that he wanted to leave Celtic. We were so lucky to have such a superb player and such a good person at the club. He was a great influence in the dressing-room and scored so many valuable goals for us that I don't think we could ever have replaced him, not even with £30 million. Arsenal have Thierry Henry; Manchester United have Ruud van Nistelrooy; Newcastle have Alan Shearer. But, honestly, I wouldn't have had any of them in my team before Henrik.

We were all dreading the summer of 2004, because we knew it was the time that he would be leaving to try something different. Deep down, we all hoped that he would perform a U-turn and stay for another year or two. If I thought that it would have made a single bit of difference, I would have gone down on bended knee and begged him to stay. The players were just as keen as everyone else to find out where he was going, and he was fed up with us asking where he would move to after Celtic. At one stage, he was so fed up with the speculation surrounding his future that he did seriously think about packing the game in and returning to Sweden for a quiet life with his wife Magdalena and their children.

Now that he's gone, we just have to get on with it. I wished him well when he left but was gutted to see him on the sidelines for so long after a great start to his Barca career. Before his knee injury, I was delighted to see him scoring regularly for Barcelona, although I'd have preferred it if he hadn't scored against us in our Champions League encounter in September 2004. Barcelona were awesome that night and defeated us 3–1.

We were really disappointed to get that campaign off to a bad start, but it was so different in 2001. We were on a real high after our 1–0 win over Porto. It was vital that we proved to everyone we could win in that company, and the players and management were delighted. That 45-minute spell in the dressing-room after the game was my favourite memory of the whole Champions League campaign. Victory in that game told us that we had what it took to hold our own at the highest level.

We played Rosenborg in the next game, and by that time people were expecting us to win, especially because we were at home. The pace of the match was furious, and the way the Norwegians passed and moved really surprised me. We scored in the first half thanks to a free-kick from Alan Thompson and had to be satisfied with that narrow victory. The win put us on top of the section, but we knew there was still a long way to go and that nothing was settled yet.

Our next challenge was away to Porto. In the build-up to the match, the manager continually told us to learn from the mistakes of our last away game in Europe against Juventus. That defeat was one huge learning curve for us, and we had to use it to our advantage. We thought we had learned that mistakes get punished, but we obviously didn't learn well enough, because silly errors were punished in the next two away games to Porto and Rosenborg.

You Can Call Me Stan

It was so frustrating, but we didn't deserve anything from the game against Porto. They won 3–0 and deserved it. It was a wake-up call, and we had to bounce back in the next game to keep our fate in our own hands. Nuno Capucho played really well that night, and I think that Alex McLeish signed him for Rangers 20 months later on the strength of his performance against us. At the time, I thought that Capucho would be a sensational signing and would enjoy a successful career in Scotland, but it wasn't to be. I was surprised that it didn't work out for him and know from chatting to him over a coffee in Glasgow one afternoon towards the end of his stay that he was also puzzled at the way things turned out.

Our next trip was away to Rosenborg, and we were still being tipped to win in Trondheim. It was so cold in Norway, way below freezing, and the pitch was really hard. It was almost impossible to play football on. The Rosenborg players obviously liked it that way, but I found it difficult to keep my feet and picked up a booking.

We were two goals down at half-time, one of them coming from former Celtic striker Harald Brattbakk. We tried to pull it back but had no luck. We created so many chances but just couldn't hit the back of the net.

I never thought that I'd hear myself say that I was glad to get back to Glasgow for the heat but it was a relief to get home! However, I didn't manage to get any sleep that night and sat up going through the 90 minutes in my head. It hit me that qualification was now out of our hands and that we needed a miracle to go through. We had to beat Juventus at home, and Rosenborg had to win in Porto.

We gave it our best shot against the Italian side, but it wasn't enough to take us through – Rosenborg were beaten 1–0 by Porto, demoting Celtic to third place in the group table. The fans backed us until they were hoarse, and we tried to do it for them, more than anything else. Goals from Joos Valgaeren, Henrik Larsson and two from Chris Sutton gave us a thrilling 4–3 victory. Sutty's goal from a volley was exceptional, even better than Del Piero's free-kick. But it was the performance of Lubo Moravcik that was the most pleasing aspect of that night. He knew it was more than likely going to be his last appearance in the Champions League and wanted to go out with a bang. He did that all right! Lubo ran the show all over the pitch and even managed to trick Pavel Nedved with a cheeky nutmeg! I really wish that he'd been just three or four years younger so that he'd still be around now, but, sadly, his time at Celtic is over, and, just like Henrik, we will *never* replace him.

He ran his old legs into the ground that night for over an hour, and I came on to replace him in the second half. He rightly received a standing ovation, and when I was waiting on the touchline to come on, I felt like joining in with the fans with their 'We're not worthy' gestures. I was a little disappointed not to start that game but wasn't even 1 per cent jealous that it was Lubo that I made way for. He deserved to play on that stage.

I remember how sad I was when he quit the club in the summer of 2002, and I only wish he had left us with another Scottish Cup winner's medal in his collection, but we lost that final 3–2 to Rangers. I felt like crying when he departed because I had lost a good friend and Celtic had lost an incredible talent. He had always said that he would go when he did, but everyone in the dressing-room thought that he would relent. By leaving when he did, he gave up the chance of one more season in Europe and the opportunity to make it three league victories in a row.

I used to go for lunch with the great man quite a lot and didn't like to go on about it all the time, but I did more or less beg him to stay because he was so important to the team. I must have got on his nerves because he stopped dining with me! But we keep in touch, and I know Celtic has a special place in his heart. He left to go to Japan for six months, and it was unfortunate that he picked up an injury that ended his career after playing for JEF United only a handful of times.

It was a big disappointment to go out of the Champions League, but we had given it everything and knew that we'd be better prepared the following season. It takes time and practice to get it right at that level. In the end, the fact that we didn't take a single point away from home cost us. However, Arsenal qualified from their section with nine points – the same amount that we finished up with – so that shows how tough our group was. But we will get there eventually. And, hopefully, sooner than some people might think.

When I think back to that whole experience I feel so proud, but I also end up feeling more and more admiration for Paul Lambert, who won the competition with Borussia Dortmund in 1997. He was superb throughout their whole campaign and deserves enormous credit, because unless you've actually been out there and played in that tournament at any stage, you'll never have a clue of the mental and physical exhaustion involved. There is no comparison between the Champions League and domestic football – it's night and day.

The concentration level required is incredible. You always have to be on your guard to prevent a counter-attack, and it is important to make sure that the best players in the opposition side see as little of the ball as possible. It is also much more physical than the SPL, and all of the opposing teams have strong players. It takes three days for your legs to recover and the same amount of time for your brain. Your body and mind are completely and utterly wrecked after every gruelling 90 minutes.

If you look at the statistics, we won every domestic game that we played immediately after a European tie. I'm still amazed at that record. We played ten and won them all – including two against Rangers – and scored twenty-seven goals and conceded just *five*. That is an incredible achievement – just ask any team that's played at that level in Europe.

However, the exertion required to play in the Champions League does eventually take its toll. Later on that season, there were instances after games when our team bus looked like an accident and emergency unit with many of the players nursing injuries and sitting with ice packs on different parts of their bodies. The fact that none of us pulled out of games unless it was absolutely impossible for us to lace up our boots demonstrates the team spirit and the desire to keep the club at the top that we have at Celtic.

After going out of the Champions League we won the right to enter the UEFA Cup. We drew Valencia, arguably the toughest team in the hat after they had reached and lost the Champions League final the two years previously. The first game was in Spain, and it was an intimidating atmosphere in the Mestalla Stadium. We were apprehensive about the first leg but knew we couldn't sit back and let them take the initiative from start to finish.

We had to believe that we were capable of taking a decent result back to Parkhead for the return leg. A 1–0 defeat was just that. Mind you, if it hadn't been for big Rab Douglas we would have lost by at least four. He was superb.

I had a good chance in the first half and so did big John. I lost my footing when Henrik put me through for my golden opportunity. I thought that their keeper was going to bring me down for a penalty, but he didn't touch me, and the chance had gone. It wasn't the last I would see of the Valencia goalkeeper Santiago Cañizares.

We came face to face again in the return leg during the penalty shoot-out after we had won 1–0 thanks to yet another brilliant goal from that man Larsson. It was going fine for us in the shoot-out up to a point. Paul Lambert and Alan Thompson had scored our first two kicks, and they had missed one, but Henrik missed our third, and I missed our fourth.

When I hit my effort high and wide, I felt every bone in my body rattle inside of me, and I struggled for breath. For a second, I thought I was going to collapse. The stadium was in complete silence, and it's hard to explain exactly what was going through my mind. I regained my composure and my breathing sufficiently to make the long walk back to the halfway line. I didn't have the courage to look my teammates in the eye – I felt that I had badly let them down. However, they told me not to worry, that we're all in it together and that these things happen in football.

Despite the setback, the shoot-out reached sudden death: Chris

Sutton scored for us and big Rab saved their fifth kick. We had a great chance of going through. Hartson netted the sixth and they scored their next. Big Joos was next up, but Cañizares saved his kick. We were then given a lifeline when the referee ordered a re-take, but, unbelievably, the keeper saved it again. We needed Rab to come up trumps once more, but it wasn't to be, and Mista scored to give them a 5–4 penalty shoot-out victory. We were totally devastated as we felt like we deserved to progress to the next round.

It was hard to take, but I think penalty shoot-outs are a necessary evil. They make the world of football go round. I'll take another one if the chance comes around again, I'm sure of that. It was another sad ending, but there's no doubt that we enhanced our reputation with that performance and proved we had some of what is required to cut it at that level.

In my first season under John Barnes, we got through the early rounds of the UEFA Cup but crashed out against French side Lyon. Maybe we would have fared better if Henrik hadn't broken his leg in the match over there, but we'll never know. The next season, when Martin O'Neill arrived, we won a couple of ties against mediocre opposition in the same competition. However, the big test came in a game against Bordeaux, another French side. We picked up a 1–1 away draw after Henrik scored with a penalty, and it gave us a great chance of going through to the next round, but they beat us 2–1 at Parkhead.

In the 2001–02 season we played at a different level again and picked up some great results – we were not as naive and were more aware of what was now required. Much of that was down to Martin O'Neill. I simply don't believe that we would have managed to beat Juventus, Porto and Rosenborg if John Barnes had still been in charge. Martin had a sensational impact for Celtic in European competition, taking the club beyond Christmas twice. Before he arrived, it had been more than 20 years since that had happened, which was embarrassing for a club the size of Celtic.

We won the league in 2002 but still had one qualifying game to play to get into the group stages of the Champions League. Swiss champions FC Basel were our opponents, and we were all satisfied with the draw. As usual there was an electric atmosphere inside Parkhead for the first leg, but within a couple of minutes, the stadium was silent after Christian Giminez scored for the Swiss side. It was a dreadful start, but we were used to setbacks, and the game was on our patch. We were back in it a few minutes later when Marco Zwyssig brought me down for a penalty after Henrik had played me in with a perfectly weighted pass. Henrik kept his nerve and drilled his spot-kick past Pascal Zuberbühler to make it 1–1.

Basel played some great stuff and could have gone ahead. To be honest they were better than I'd expected. Hakan Yakin, in particular, caused us all sorts of problems playing behind the front two. But we had the desire and the guts to get in front. We went 2–1 ahead when Sutton cleverly deflected a Neil Lennon shot past the keeper. We could have gone further ahead when we were awarded another penalty after Murat Yakin handled, but Zuberbühler saved Henrik's powerful shot with his left leg. Not scoring that penalty was a blow, as a one-goal lead is never enough to take to the away leg in European competition. Thankfully, we kept plugging away and got the third that we so wanted on 86 minutes when Momo Sylla scored with a spectacular volley after he got on the end of a Steve Guppy cross. It gave us the cushion that we desired, but it still wasn't enough.

We travelled to Switzerland for the return. It's a beautiful country with really friendly people, and I'd like to go back there on a family holiday sometime in the future. However, the game itself was a nightmare for us. We never looked organised and couldn't get into our stride. We were a goal down after eight minutes when Giminez scored again. Hakan Yakin pulled the strings once more, and we couldn't come up with the answer as to how to stop him.

His brother Murat made it 2–0 after 22 minutes, and we didn't look like recovering after that. Basel went through on the away goals rule after the tie finished 3–3. We had a couple of chances to score, but it was a weak performance from us that night. We were out of the Champions League before the competition had even started. It was a crushing blow. The journey home was a quiet one. No words were spoken. It was one of the most depressing atmospheres I've ever known during my time with Celtic. I hate nights like that. The only thing that came out of it was that we retained a UEFA Cup spot and embarked on that great run to Seville.

Because we didn't win the league in 2002–03, we had to play two qualifying rounds to make it into the Champions League for the 2003–04 season. We faced FBK Kaunas in the first qualifying round and had to travel to Lithuania for the first leg. We won 4–0, Henrik, Sutty, Shaun Maloney and Liam Miller scoring the goals. A lot of players were rested for the second leg, but we won 1–0 thanks to an own goal from Darius Gvildys. The first game had been surrounded by sadness as Kaunas striker Audrius Slekys died in a car crash three days before the match. It was tragic.

The draw for the second qualifying round was kind to us, and we were paired against MTK Hungaria. It was a tricky tie, but we got an excellent result in the first leg when we won 4–0 away. I scored that night along with Larsson, Agathe and Sutton. Henrik's goal was his 31st in UEFA competition for Celtic and made him the highest ever scorer for a British side in Europe. Peter Lorimer and Ian Rush held the record before him.

In the return leg, we took it easy and won 1–0 thanks to Chris Sutton. It was Celtic's 100th European game at Parkhead that night, and we celebrated by getting into the Champions League – the stage we all craved. The draw put us into Group A along with Bayern Munich, Lyon and Anderlecht. It wasn't a bad draw, and we felt we had an excellent chance of progressing to the next phase. All we had to do was finish in the top two to create our own little piece of Celtic history.

Our first game was in Munich at the Olympic Stadium. Bayern – under Ottmar Hitzfeld – had suffered a poor season in Europe the previous year, not winning a single game. However, they had cruised to their domestic championship and had spent £13 million to sign Dutch striker Roy Makaay from Deportivo La Coruña. He was a man that we knew could score goals at that level.

They had us under pressure in the first half, but we made sure we kept our discipline and shape. Bayern kept coming at us looking for a goal, and we knew gaps would be left in their half which we had to exploit. On the 57-minute mark, Henrik raced away from Bixente Lizarazu down the right wing and fed Didier. He crossed to the back post, and Thommo was waiting to head home from a tight angle past Oliver Kahn. Bayern were stunned, and, if I am honest, we might also have been a little surprised.

They threw everything at us to get back into the game, and it looked as though we were going to hold out for one of the finest results in Celtic's history, but we blew it in the closing minutes. From a Bayern cross, Stan Varga's header reached the edge of the area, and Makaay was waiting to send a powerful shot past Magnus Hedman. We would have settled for a point but suffered a killer blow right at the end when Makaay swung over a cross from the right. Michael Ballack couldn't get his head on it, but it went over everyone, bounced just in front of Magnus and flew up into the net. It was a freak goal but should have been prevented. The manager was raging about it in the dressing-room after the game.

It crushed us and we were under pressure going into the next game, at home to Lyon. We had to win. They were a brilliant side. They played attractive football, zipping the ball about the pitch, and their passing and moving was wonderful. They had Giovane Elber and Vikash Dhorasoo in their team but couldn't convert their possession and pressure into goals.

Alan Thompson missed a penalty in the first half, but we recovered and got a grip of the game in the second 45 minutes. Like many teams before them, Lyon found out just how resilient we were on our own patch. We hated losing at Parkhead. We opened the scoring through Liam Miller on 70 minutes. His goal came at the end of a 21- or 22-pass move – a passing sequence that I was proud to have been a part of. The previous four seasons in Europe had taught us plenty. We knew we had to keep the ball, keep the ball and then explode into attacking action when the time was right. With this in mind, we were patient in the build-up to Miller's goal, passing the ball about the pitch. Lyon were chasing shadows. The move ended with Henrik sending over a perfect cross that Liam met with his head to bullet home past Grégory Coupet. It was one of the finest goals Celtic Park has ever seen, and I think it's one of the best that I've ever been involved in. Sutton then rounded off a great night when he headed home another fantastic delivery from Henrik.

For our next challenge, we were back on our travels, away to Belgian champs Anderlecht. I was confident that we'd get at least a draw but wasn't going to be happy unless we won. It turned out that we got neither and were dumped to our fifth straight defeat away from home in the Champions League. Were we ever going to learn?

They were a man down after 25 minutes when their captain Glen de Boek was sent off after he received two yellow cards. We were in control from then on but missed a few chances. Hartson also had a goal disallowed for offside. We paid the price when Aruna Dindane scored for them on 71 minutes. We tried to level it, but it was never going to happen.

Anderlecht came to our place two weeks later, and we wanted to teach them a lesson after the disappointments of the first game. And we did. We played some great football and went at them straight from kick-off. We were three up within half an hour. The whole team played with style and terrific pace. Henrik, Miller and Sutty scored the goals, but big John played really well and had a hand in all three. They scored in the second half when Dindane slammed home the rebound after Magnus had saved his penalty.

That win had us right back in it, and we were determined to beat Bayern when they came to Parkhead. They defended well, happy to play for a point, and left satisfied after a 0–0 draw.

That result left us top of the section, and only a point was needed from our final game for us to make it through to the next stage. We were off to Lyon, which I wasn't comfortable about. Remembering how well they had played at Parkhead, I wasn't over confident that we'd get the result that we required. My fears were confirmed when we went a goal down after just five minutes. Juninho's free-kick crashed off the crossbar and fell to Elber, who nodded the loose ball past Hedman.

They should have scored two or three more, but we were hanging in there, defending for our lives. However, in the 23rd minute we equalized thanks to a goal from big John. Sutton headed down my cross, which should have been cleared, but Claudio Caçapa got his feet in a muddle and John pounced to side foot home. It was 1–1 at the break, and the manager urged us to keep it tight for the first ten minutes after the restart and then gain some momentum to attack them. Unfortunately, our plans were in tatters a few minutes later when Magnus allowed a shot from Juninho to bounce over him and into the net. So, we were back to square one. It was soul destroying to get back into games only to then hit the self-destruct button.

We had to lift ourselves, though, and we were at Lyon again. Momo Sylla worked hard to close down Edmilson, and the Brazilian's attempted clearance ended up in his own penalty area. As others hesitated, Sutton pounced to slide home the equalizer. We were through. Well, at least for a few minutes until they scored again. Bobo handled a cross inside the box, and Juninho scored from the resultant penalty. Our chance of going through to the last 16 was gone.

At the end of games like that one, you come off the pitch wondering if it's all worth it. It must have been worse for a few of the guys who knew that it might have been their last chance of really doing something memorable in the Champions League. For example, it was Henrik's last season with us. That night must have left him angry and frustrated. We all were, I suppose. Also, the fact that, for whatever reasons, we hadn't brought in two or three players of real quality to improve the squad in the weeks after Seville came back to haunt us that night.

You Can Call Me Stan

The only consolation was that we finished third in the group and had the UEFA Cup to fall back on. FK Teplice stood between us and the last 16 of that tournament, and we managed to dispose of them fairly comfortably. We won the first leg at home 3–0, two goals coming from Henrik and the other from Chris.

The away leg in the Czech Republic was always going to be tricky, and we made hard work of it. The stadium wasn't great; the changing rooms were even worse. It was a cold, dark night and we lost 1–0, the match only going ahead after a 30-minute power cut. At one stage it looked as though the match was going to have to be cancelled – it would have been played the following afternoon instead – but it didn't come to that. Jiří Mašek scored their winning goal in the first half. We weren't pleased at losing, but in games such as those, it's all about getting in and out with your name still in the draw for the next round.

And what a draw it was. We had been pulled out of the hat along with Barcelona, which meant that we were up against one of the biggest clubs in the world. It was great stuff. The first leg was at Parkhead, and it was a night of madness and mayhem. Rab was sent off by referee Wolfgang Stark in the tunnel following an incident with Thiago Motta at half-time. It was 0–0 at that stage, and with Magnus on loan at Italian side Ancona, it meant that young David Marshall was handed his competitive debut. I think that he would have expected to be busier, but he had a fairly quiet 45 minutes. What he did have to do, he handled comfortably.

Javier Saviola was sent off for Barca midway through the second half, and we went on to record a memorable victory. On the hour, I sent in a cross from the right, and Henrik got up to beat the magnificent Carlos Puyol in the air to cushion a header down for Thompson. Alan kept his composure and volleyed the ball past Victor Valdés.

We survived some scary moments but couldn't be denied the win. Stephen Pearson is due a lot of credit for his performance that night as he played wonderfully well. He had joined us only a couple of months earlier from Motherwell, but he terrorised

Michael Reiziger with his direct play, so much so that the Dutch defender was subbed for his own protection by Barca boss Frank Rijkaard.

Still, we knew we had a mountain to climb in the next leg. David Marshall was still in goal, because Rab Douglas was suspended, and we had John Kennedy partnering Stan Varga in defence, because Bobo Balde was also banned. I talked to Hristo Stoichkov before the game in the Nou Camp, and he told me that he expected Celtic to lose by four goals. Naturally, I disagreed with him, even though we had some young and inexperienced players in our team.

Ronaldinho was the man we had to keep an eye on. Then again, Xavi, Luis García and Philip Cocu couldn't exactly be ignored. Barca cut us open a few times in the early stages, as was inevitable, but David Marshall got himself in the way of everything. It was a night for giving your lot, and we all managed to put in a superb shift to secure a 0–0 draw.

David Marshall and John Kennedy were an inspiration to us. David didn't look back after making a great diving save at the feet of Gerard inside the first minute, and John's positional play was excellent. Chris Sutton and Henrik Larsson defended from the front, and we had two strong banks of four behind them.

After the game, the manager gave special thanks to David and John, and rightly so. David, in particular, was unbelievable that night. For a 19 year old to play so well in that environment, under that pressure, was incredible. It was a great night to be a Celtic player. I only wish that I had made a decent bet with Stoichkov!

After our win over Barcelona, we knew we had to play Spanish side Villarreal. They weren't the sexiest name in the Primera Liga but a team full of talented players, nonetheless. We were fairly confident, although I did wonder if we had used up all our good fortune in the previous round against Barca. Still, that didn't stop many people from saying that we were going to be in Gothenburg for the UEFA Cup final on 19 May. A lot of fans already had their flights and accommodation booked. Newcastle were also in the last eight, and many people hoped that the two British sides could meet in the final.

You Can Call Me Stan

The first leg against Villarreal was at home – a scenario that we had become used to. The commonly held belief is that it is better to be away first, and I agree with that, but being at home didn't seem to be doing us any harm considering our achievements in the previous 18 months. Villarreal came to our place in a confident mood and played some good stuff. We couldn't get going and were 1–0 down at half-time. Their goal came after I was fouled just outside their box, but referee Kyros Vassaras waved play on. They broke up the park and won a corner. From the resulting kick, Josico scored with a looping header over Marshall. To be honest, Villarreal could have scored two or three more in that opening forty-five minutes. They had good movement and pulled us all over the place.

But we knew the situation and that our time in the game would come. We had a goal disallowed when Henrik charged down a clearance from keeper José Reina, and the ball ended up in the net. The ref was having none of it and chalked it off as he felt Henrik had used an arm. That decision fired us up. The atmosphere created by our fans was brilliant, and we had a couple of near misses. We equalized on 64 minutes when Didier delivered a good cross into the box, and Henrik was there to nod home. He even had a chance to grab a winner but couldn't capitalize on the opportunity.

The second leg was always going to be tough. It was a hot night inside their little stadium on the outskirts of Valencia. We were dealt a blow when Chris Sutton ruled himself out with an injury, in the hours leading up to kick-off. Things went from bad to worse, and we never got into our stride. For the first time in a long time, there appeared to be a lack of confidence on the pitch from the Celtic team. Villarreal sensed our trepidation and took full advantage. Sonny Anderson scored in the first half, and Roger scored after the interval. They deserved to win. Absolutely.

It was simply a tie too far for us. We had given our all in European football for the previous year and a half, and there was just nothing left to give. Not a single drop. Their keeper didn't have a single save of any note to make. We ran out of energy. We ran out of ideas. We ran out of inspiration. The players and the manager knew that kind of night would come, and that's why we had needed to strengthen the team properly in the summer after we had made it to Seville.

If we thought that was bad, our next venture into Europe was so disappointing. We were given a nightmare draw for the Champions League in the 2004–05 season when we were placed in a group with AC Milan, Barcelona and Shakhtar Donetsk. Yes, there is excitement when such glamorous teams come out of the glass bowl at the UEFA headquarters, but there's also a feeling that the draw could have been kinder.

On top of the difficult draw, we also faced European competition for the first time without Henrik, who, ironically, had joined Barca that summer. Barcelona came to Parkhead on 15 September and had strengthened their side from the previous season. As well as having to contend with the loss of Henrik Larsson and the fact that he was now playing against us, they had also signed Deco, Ludovic Giuly and Samuel Eto'o. Despite our terrific home record in Europe – we hadn't lost at Celtic Park for over three years – they were the favourites, and it was really no surprise that they came and defeated us comfortably.

Barca's first-half display was terrific. It was hard to get close to them as they sprayed the ball about the park. It was the kind of performance that could be used to teach young kids about the way football should be played. Deco scored with a shot from a tight angle, which put them ahead at the interval. David Marshall then continued his heroics against Barca when he saved a penalty from Ronaldinho to stop us going two down. That gave us a boost and our supporters a huge lift.

We responded, and Chris Sutton scored after an hour when he turned a Henri Camara cross into the net. We were on the up and deserved to equalize. We had a grip on the game at that point and Didier was flying. Frank Rijkaard, the Barca boss, responded by taking off Eto'o and replacing him with Andrés Iniesta to help tighten his side up. He also took off Ronaldinho and replaced him with Henrik.

At that stage of the game I think Rijkaard would have settled for a draw, but his team is full of quality, and they scored a second when Henrik laid the ball off to Juliano Belletti, whose cross was tucked away by Giuly. Henrik then scored their third after he intercepted a Thompson headed back pass to round Marshall and put the ball in the back of the net. It was strange to see him score against us. We all still wanted him to be wearing the Celtic jersey.

When you lose a game like that you hope to have an easier 90 minutes the next time you play in the Champions League, to give you a chance of getting some points on the board. Sadly, we had to travel to Italy to play AC Milan, one of the tournament favourites. Once again, as had happened so often in the previous season's Champions League campaign, we lost late goals to kill us off. We also got off to a bad start and were a goal down inside seven minutes when Andriy Shevchenko scored. We battled hard to keep them from scoring another, and the never-say-die attitude of Martin O'Neill's side came to the fore again when Stan Varga got above Paolo Maldini and Alessandro Nesta to head home my corner. However, Milan had the luxury of having Pippo Inzaghi and Rui Costa on the bench. Both of them came on in the second half, and it was Inzaghi who scored their second with a little over a minute to go. We couldn't believe it. It was another painful lesson to be learned. Why were we losing so many late goals in Europe? It was a question that was to often haunt us during that season – worryingly, it happened far too often in domestic games as well. To rub salt in our wounds, Andrea Pirlo scored their third with a deflected free-kick in injury time, but the game was already over by that point.

There's no doubt that our heads were down when we played Shakhtar Donetsk, and, looking back, it's no surprise that we lost 3–0 in Ukraine. We were never in the game, and it was one of those nights when nothing went right for us. Francelino Matuzalém scored twice, and Brandão scored their third. There's not much to be said about that game. I was embarrassed by our performance. I felt very low – we all did. We had no points from three games, and there was a fear that we'd end up with the same amount of points after the group section had finished. We had to lift ourselves.

Shakhtar came to our place, and we managed to get our first points on the board. Alan Thompson scored the only goal of the game on 24 minutes. The Ukrainian side had two players sent off that night and still caused us problems when they were down to nine men. We were so relieved to get three points. The win left us with a chance of making third place and qualification for the UEFA Cup.

Our next game took us back to the Nou Camp, and we were being tipped to lose by three or four goals. However, having drawn 0–0 at their stadium in the UEFA Cup the previous season, there was a bit of belief that we could pull something off again. And we did, drawing 1–1. If only we could play all our away games there!

We had gone to Spain on the back of a league defeat to Rangers at Ibrox only to find out that Lubos Michel was to be the referee. The Slovakian had been heavily criticised for the way that he handled our UEFA Cup final against Porto, and we were not keen to see him again. That night, Ronaldinho played well but found it difficult to get the better of big Joos. Didier also played fantastically. Samuel Eto'o scored for them in the first half but we fought back again, and Hartson equalized just before the break. We were right up against it in the second half but held out for another great result at the Nou Camp. For once we didn't concede a late goal, and our efforts were properly rewarded. The draw in Barcelona gave us our first point in the Champions League away from home after nine attempts. Around 9,000 of our fans were inside the stadium that night, and it was great to give them something to cheer about.

Henrik had been ruled out of the game that night with a knee injury but made his way down to our dressing-room after the game to see us all. Hobbling around on his crutches, he said that he was delighted to see us grab a point. His heart was very much still with Celtic, not that I was ever in any doubt about that.

Although we were out of the Champions League, we were still in with a great chance of finishing third in the section as we were a point ahead of Shakhtar. They were at home to Barcelona in their final game, and we were hosting Milan. Henrik had assured us that he would urge his teammates to beat Shakhtar and help us stay in Europe, but Rijkaard's side couldn't do it and lost in the sub-zero temperature of Ukraine. We drew 0–0 against Milan and played really well. Aiden McGeady had a storming match against the Italian side. They knew nothing about him before kick-off but had two men marking him after 15 minutes. Unfortunately, we just couldn't turn our possession into goals.

The curtain came down on us that night. It was the first time in three appearances in the Champions League that we had finished bottom of our group and had fallen out of European competition altogether. After the great times we had enjoyed in recent seasons, I suppose we couldn't complain too much. However, we can't rest on what has happened in the past. Seville was great and will live with us all until our last moments, but we should always be looking to progress. Standing still, or going back the way, should not be on the agenda for a club the size of Celtic.

We thought that things couldn't get any worse after coming last in our group in the Champions League in the 2004–05 . . . then along came Artmedia Bratislava. The draw for the second qualifying round of the Champions League in the 2005–06 season looked to have been kind to us, and we were delighted to be going to Slovakia for the first leg. It was our first competitive game since losing the league title at Motherwell on the last day of the previous season, and it was also Gordon Strachan's first meaningful game as manager. The gaffer and the team wanted to send out a message that despite the change of manager we were still a force in Europe. Instead, it ended in disaster: we lost the first leg in Bratislava 5–0. As I walked off the park that night, I felt totally embarrassed and humiliated. I'm sure I wasn't the only one. Some of our travelling fans showed their disgust towards the players and management as we left the pitch, and they were definitely entitled to do so. It was Celtic's worst ever result in European competition, and I felt so low to be a part of it. We gave our all in the return leg six days later and won 4–0. Alan Thompson, John Hartson, Stephen McManus and Craig Beattie scored the goals. It was a good effort but just not enough to take us through.

It was an awful feeling to be out of Europe at such an early stage of the season. For a few moments after the return leg at Celtic Park, I felt like all that we had built up in the previous five years had been for nothing. How could we go from such highs to the biggest low of all?

I felt particularly sorry for Neil Lennon. I've got a really good relationship with Neil and know how much being appointed Jackie McNamara's successor as club captain meant to him. He desperately wanted us to have a good season; he wanted to be leading us out on those special Champions League nights. Neil only signed a one-year extension to his contract, and the 2005–06 season could be his last. After everything he's had to put up with on and off the park during his time with Celtic, he deserved much more than that lousy game against Artmedia Bratislava.

11

Euro 2004

I had genuine hopes that Bulgaria could be the dark horses of Euro 2004. I'm not saying I expected us to go to Portugal and win the tournament, but I thought we could progress to the semi-final stage, as the team had managed to do in the 1994 World Cup in the USA. Sadly, my optimism couldn't have been proved more wrong.

We finished our qualifying section in top spot and played some fabulous football in the 20-month campaign to get to the finals. Confidence was high in our camp. We had come through a difficult group to finish ahead of Belgium and Croatia, and, to be honest, the players and supporters were a little surprised at our success. When the initial qualifying draw had been made we didn't think that we had much of a chance because Bulgaria hadn't been doing well for a few years. The last time that we had made it to a major championship was Euro 96 in England.

Before the tournament began, I had been appointed as captain of Bulgaria, taking over from legendary midfielder Krassi Balakov. During his career, he had been an inspiration to us all. We badly missed his experience in Portugal, and I think that his absence played a huge part in the team finishing bottom of a group that included Sweden, Denmark and Italy. He had retired from international football because he felt as if he could give nothing else to the team. The players believed that he was still contributing, but it was his decision, and I respected it.

When we qualified for Portugal, I was so pleased for the Bulgarian fans that we had given them something to cheer about. For years the team had been in the doldrums. It was so desperate that in one of our World Cup 2002 qualifiers we played in front of just 1,500 fans in Sofia against the Czech Republic. Our fans had abandoned us, and it was really hard to take. But when the good times returned so did our supporters, and a few thousand of them travelled to Portugal to cheer us on.

Our opening game was against Sweden in Lisbon's José Alvalade XXI stadium. It was my 113th competitive game in two seasons. At times during that mammoth run, I felt mentally and physically exhausted but was desperate to play in the finals. I wanted to be part of it more than I wanted to be lying on a beach, taking it easy with a beer.

Plamen Markov was our manager at the time, and he invited Hristo Stoichkov and Krassi Balakov to travel with the official party. He wanted to use their experience and have them around our hotel base and training camp to offer advice and encouragement. I enjoyed playing under Markov but was frustrated that he played me as a sitting midfielder. I wanted to be the box-to-box man but rarely got the chance to do that for my country. However, I was not going to make an issue of it, especially as I was the captain. As usual, I decided to give it my all, whatever the position. I always try to ensure that when my opponents come off the pitch they remember me as someone they won't look forward to facing again.

It's an honour to be captain of my country but, away from playing, the hassle that comes with the job is something I'd rather not have to deal with. The build-up to Euro 2004 was riddled with problems that I had to contend with on behalf of the players and our families. I was involved in negotiations with the Bulgarian FA over bonus and sponsorship payments for players. I also had to make sure that the wives of all the boys had decent accommodation and transport during their stay in Portugal.

Because I'm not based in Bulgaria, I only got the chance to really sit down and negotiate when I was back in the country on international duty. A lot of my time was spent meeting officials, and the strain left me tired and frustrated. I wasn't just negotiating for a deal I was happy with – I had to achieve a compromise that suited more than 20 players. It was something that proved difficult. Some players were happy with things that others wouldn't be happy with, and it became a bit of a stressful situation for me.

After much talking, we were eventually able to reach an agreement that everyone was happy with, but it was a strain that I could have done without in the lead-up to finals. If we ever qualify for another major tournament, I hope that the negotiations for payments are much smoother, because I don't know if I could go through all that again. I am with Bulgaria to play football, not to be a cross between an agent and a lawyer. However, the reason that I decided to keep negotiating was to make everyone happy because I'm a team player on and off the park. I'd hate to have it on my conscience if I let anyone down.

Being captain is all about taking responsibility every minute of every day. Balakov told me that it wouldn't be just about putting on the armband and tossing the coin, and he has been proved right. Captaincy has had its problems, but it's been helpful that he's made himself available to chat, and he has given me one or two bits of advice when I've asked him to. The decisions that I make as captain will not always be right, and I have made the wrong calls once or twice, but I am young, I am trying my best and I am learning about the role every day.

Before heading to Portugal to our base in Varzim near the coast, we spent about 11 days in Sofia. The nights spent with the team in the build-up to a major competition can be boring, but Markov made sure that we had one or two evenings of entertainment lined up. We went to the cinema, and he brought in a comedian on another occasion. We also had a day off to attend Vladimir Manchev's wedding in Sofia.

I remember reading articles in the past from players involved in World Cups and European Championships, and they talked about how boredom set in and caused friction in the camp. Roy Keane, for example, cited boredom – along with a lack of proper facilities – as part of the reason for his walking out of the Republic of Ireland squad in the Japan and South Korea 2002 World Cup finals. England players Sol Campbell and Michael Owen have said that they found it difficult to keep their minds occupied in that tournament, so far away from home. As captain I looked upon it as my duty to make sure that we had activities to keep us busy. I had a meeting with Markov, and we came up with a list of events for the squad. Other players also had an input to ensure that all tastes were catered for. Table tennis featured highly on our list of non-football activities.

I like my teammates, but sometimes enough can be enough. I need my own space when I am at a training camp with the national side. I get particularly annoyed when my fellow countrymen criticise Scottish football. In Bulgaria I'm often asked if the SPL is enough for me, and I always say that it is. Right now, I don't feel the need to go anywhere else. Those who question the quality of football in Scotland are ignorant. People think it is easy to win games in the Premier League, but it's definitely not. It is tough to win, especially away from home. For example, our 77-game unbeaten home run wasn't an easy thing to achieve and we were made to work hard for it.

In the friendly games leading up to the tournament, we didn't look too good defensively. Our level of concentration was poor, and we didn't defend as a unit. Things didn't improve, and we ended up losing our opening game against Sweden, which was refereed by Scottish whistler Stuart Dougal. But we didn't just lose – it was more than just a defeat. We were thrashed 5–0, Henrik scoring two fabulous goals. Our performance was a total embarrassment, and I was ashamed as I walked off the pitch at the humiliating defeat.

I was on a downer and things went from bad to worse in our second game when we lost 1–0 to Denmark to send us out of the tournament before we'd even played our final match. I was sent off for two bookable offences. At the time I was red carded – and still to this day – I was sure that the Portuguese referee Lucilio Batista didn't mean to send me off. I was booked on 77 minutes for a foul on Tomas Gravesen and then received a second yellow five minutes later for dissent. We were denied a clear free-kick at the edge of Denmark's area when Zdravko Lazarov was brought down. The ref waved away our claims, and as soon as play stopped, I ran up to him to let him know what I thought. I was frustrated and angry at the way things were going. I am a bad loser. Also, I'd taken injections before the game to numb the pain on a knee injury and didn't go through that hardship just for the ref to spoil it.

As I was running up to him, he had his yellow card in the air to book Marian Hristov. I shouted to the referee that his decision was a joke. My exact words were, 'That's a f****** joke.' It is the kind of thing that's said to refs in every game from amateur football to the very highest level. I didn't call him a w***** or a p****. I wouldn't do that because as much as I might not agree with the decisions referees make, I still respect them.

Usually the captain is allowed to speak to the ref to make his team's feelings known. Referees and captains have that kind of relationship on the pitch, or at least they should have. But the ref didn't see who was shouting at him, he just heard the words, and because he had the card in the air, he automatically turned his body and waved the yellow at the 'voice' that he had heard. When he realised who it was I think he regretted it, although he didn't tell me that at the time. Despite my disappointment, I accepted his decision. I shook the referee's hand and said thank you and good luck to him. I wasn't being sarcastic, I meant it. I never forget my manners.

I think that referees have to be more understanding. They have to appreciate that players are nervous and highly charged during games, and there has to be some consideration. Inconsistent refereeing can't continue to spoil tournaments. I also reckon the so-called bigger nations more often get the benefit of the doubt from referees. Maybe if it had been France or Portugal looking for that free-kick at the edge of the box the referee would have awarded it.

After losing 5–0 to Sweden, it was important to bounce back against Denmark, and I was desperate to do well against them. I wanted to win the game and give us a chance of qualifying for the quarter-finals. However, because I was told by Markov to play as a defensive midfielder, I didn't get the chance to attack as often as I would have liked. My priority was to protect our defence. I found my defensive role very frustrating, as it went against my natural instincts. In my opinion, it took away the best part of my game. I am most effective when I am bursting forward and hurting the opposition by scoring goals, creating chances, winning free-kicks in the final third or freeing up space for others to score.

I thought long and hard about that in the build-up to the Denmark match and decided to go and speak to Markov about it. My view on the game was that I wanted to play to win it, instead of just trying to avoid defeat. I approached the boss on the morning of the match and said to him that I felt that I should be allowed to go into attacking areas. He didn't agree and told me that my job was to play as a sitting midfielder. He said that he wasn't going to change his mind. I wasn't happy, but he was the coach, and I respected his decision. He was there to hand out instructions and tell us how we were going to approach the game tactically. As captain, I could offer an opinion but couldn't go against the wishes of the manager. I was always conscious of the fact that I had to set an example to the other players, but I left the meeting feeling extremely frustrated.

I know that after our defeat to Sweden some people back in Scotland, and a few managers in the game, questioned why I wasn't attacking more. I was told that they suspected that I was being lazy because people are used to seeing me bursting from box to box in a Celtic jersey. Believe me, I wanted to burst from box to box: it's what my game is all about.

Did my frustration play a part in my red card against Denmark? Yeah, it probably did. However, I accept full responsibility for my actions. It was the first red card of my career, and it couldn't have come at a worse time. I felt really low as I walked off the pitch that night, because I had let people down. For the tournament to end in that manner was shattering. It left me feeling depressed and dejected. I had put so much into my preparation for Euro 2004, and I don't just mean in the couple of weeks leading up to it. I started my training six months ahead of the tournament, a few days after Christmas. I think that I only had two nights out in that six-month period. I ate the right things at the proper times, rested a lot and trained harder than I had ever done before. I even neglected my family by not spending as much time with Paulina and son Stiliyan as I should have because of my commitment to getting ready for the tournament in Portugal.

Our final group game was against Italy, and it would have been my 50th international cap. However, instead of lining up against the likes of Del Piero, Vieri and Pirlo, I had to watch from the stands. The match ended in a 1–1 draw, which sent both teams out of the tournament. Markov resigned as our coach a few days later, and Hristo Stoichkov was named as his successor.

Greece won the tournament, beating Portugal in the final. I was on holiday in Greece at the time, and the celebrations were wild. At the time, I couldn't help wondering what it would have been like if my own country had gone all the way. One thing's for sure, the party in Bulgaria would have matched any nation's in the world if we'd won.

12

The National Team

I made my debut for Bulgaria in 1999 against Egypt in a three-team tournament in Cairo. I was only 19 years old and was called up more or less at the last minute after a couple of players had pulled out through injury. Hristo Stoichkov was in the squad, and it was such a thrill to know that I could be playing beside him.

To get to Egypt I had to make my own way from a CSKA training camp in Cyprus, and I was nervous about going to the Middle East on my own. Thankfully, the journey was fine, and the players and management made me feel welcome when I arrived at our training base. I played against the Egyptians for 45 minutes, and we lost 3–1.

Although I had been capped more than 20 times at Under-21 level, I was surprised to be included in the full team at such a young age. I remember phoning home to tell my family that I was going to be involved in the game. It was as good a moment as I had ever known in football – I was so proud. All my life I had wanted to play for my country, and I was thrilled when it happened for real. Sure, we lost the game and I was disappointed, but for me that night was all about pulling that jersey on and trying to turn in a good individual performance.

I performed to a decent standard on my debut and received the nod for the next game against Hong Kong. I played the full 90 minutes in a 3–1 win and also played the entire match against Mexico in a game that we lost 2–0. Dmitr Dmitrov was the coach at that point, and he was set to stay on after the tournament but had a change of heart and returned to club football. That was a huge disappointment for me, and I wondered if my international career was over after just three friendly games. But I stayed involved in the squad and the new manager handed me my competitive debut against Poland in a World Cup qualifier in 1999. Unfortunately, we lost 2–0. It wasn't the best of games for me because I missed a great opportunity to score when we were a goal down. If I had stuck that chance away who knows what might have happened.

Ever since I was a kid I wanted to play for my country. I particularly remember the team that participated in the 1994 World Cup when Stoichkov was the star player. I was about 14 years old when he was at his peak and part of that great side. The way that Bulgaria played at that time was right up there with the best in the world. I remember the reception that the team received when they returned home after that World Cup – they were greeted as national heroes. Every single player and member of the coaching staff was treated like a king. They wanted for nothing in our country and could do no wrong.

Stoichkov was an incredibly gifted player and a fantastic professional. I followed his career for years, and he was one of my idols so you can imagine how I felt when I actually got to train beside him. He used to come and practise with CSKA when he was home on holiday from Barcelona. We got to know each other at that point, and our relationship grew when I made it into the national squad. He used to teach me things on the pitch and talk to me to make sure that I was using my brain, as well as improving with the ball at my feet.

The national teams that have followed have always been

compared with that fine side of 1994, and, sometimes, it's been a tough burden to shoulder. It's not an easy task to live up to the standard that they produced, and, so far, we've failed to manage it in my time. We didn't qualify for Euro 2000 in Holland and Belgium or the 2002 World Cup finals in Japan and Korea. We did make it to Euro 2004 in Portugal but let ourselves down over there.

It all started to go wrong for Bulgaria about a year after the success of 1994, and our fans started to desert us. We had to move games from Levski's stadium to CSKA's so that the stands didn't look so empty. I could understand our fans' frustrations, as we'd let them down so many times by failing to qualify for the big tournaments.

We now have a decent side with players from many of the big leagues in Europe so we should be making the most of our qualities. We have a young team – most of the guys are 23, 24 and 25. We are maturing together, building up a great understanding on the pitch and a great team spirit off it. We have some excellent players like Georgi Peev at Dynamo Kiev, Dimitar Berbatov at Bayer Leverkusen and Martin Petrov at Atlético Madrid. We also have several other players starring in the Bundesliga and a couple in the French and Turkish leagues.

Like in Scotland, the fans are dismayed by the national team's lack of success, and we are just as frustrated as they are. We have a population of only six million in my country, but that is not an excuse. Expectations run high, and our fans aren't slow in letting us know if they're angry. Every week the radio and television phone-ins are full of unhappy callers. One night, the vitriol and criticism got so bad that I decided that I'd had enough – this time they'd gone way overboard.

We lost 6–0 to the Czech Republic in Prague in our last match of the 2002 World Cup qualifying section, and the verbal abuse got too much. We had to win that game to have a chance of qualifying, but it just didn't happen for us. We had no luck that night, and every time the Czechs touched the ball it seemed to go into the back of the net.

You Can Call Me Stan

After the game, our media asked me whether I had cried with disappointment, but there was no point in tears. Crying would not have achieved anything. I said that we had to learn from the result and immediately set about lifting our heads for the next competitive game. The media still proceeded to tear us apart and even played a funeral march over the radio as they read out the names of the 11 players who had started the game that night. Their reaction was way, way over the top.

Then a friend phoned me one night to tell me that coach Stojko Mladenov was receiving dreadful abuse on a sports programme back home. So, from my home in Glasgow I called the studio and appealed to the presenters and every viewer to get behind the manager and the players.

A few days before that I had decided that I wanted to quit the national team. I reckoned that I was wasting my time and effort. I was trying my best to make people happy and all I was getting was abuse from the fans and media. I gave my all in the 2002 World Cup campaign, but it was difficult for me as I had just recovered from my broken leg and wasn't at my best for a couple of the games.

I spoke to Mladenov about finishing with the national side, but he believed that I was too young to quit and that there were plenty of good times ahead for Bulgaria. He told me not to rush into the decision because I might regret it. For a few days, I agonised over my future in the national team, and I also spoke to my father. We had a good chat, and he made me see sense about some important things. My father reminded me that I was representing my country and had an example to set to the rest of the squad and every young Bulgarian footballer. If I ran away from the situation then what was to stop everyone else chucking it all in as well? That conversation changed my mind about quitting the national set-up, and, in hindsight, I'm glad that I didn't turn my back on my country at that time.

Now I'm fully committed and want to reach the milestone of gaining 100 caps for Bulgaria. I'm on more than 50 just now and if I stay fit and in good form on the pitch then I will achieve my goal.

Unlike Scotland players, we don't receive actual 'caps' and there is no Bulgarian Hall of Fame or anything like that, although I think there should be one for every country.

Stojko Mladenov was a real influence on my career and made me the captain when I was just 21 years old. It was a great honour, although I was surprised to get the armband ahead of some of the more experienced players like Zdravko Zdravkov. We all had to submit a list of three players that we wanted to be the captain in order of preference. Once the ballots had been counted, the manager announced that I had received the most votes. Most of the players and coaching staff congratulated me and promised me their full support, but a couple of my teammates were not happy about it. Radostin Kishishev was upset with the decision, and he decided to quit the national team. I had no problem with his reaction, and we have remained friends to this day.

I was honoured and proud when my teammates voted me to replace Balakov as captain. The extra responsibility is something that I thrive on. Of course, I'm not the perfect skipper and mistakes will be made, but Balakov told me how to deal with the negatives as well as the positives, and I appreciated his advice. I am learning all the time about the kind of responsibility that captaincy brings.

On the whole, the Bulgarian media treat me well and always make a fuss of me when I arrive from Scotland for international games. There are always dozens of newspaper journalists and radio and television crews at the airport waiting to interview me. They all want to know every single aspect of my life in Scotland and my football career at Celtic.

It's nice to go back and see my friends and family when I am on international duty, but I do wish that from a footballing point of view the Bulgarian national set-up was more professional. When I first started playing for my country we were treated like a second-rate outfit by some of the people attached to our team. For example, the training equipment wasn't up to scratch. We have a contract with Puma, but at that time we didn't seem to be getting the same quality of gear as other countries that have their kit supplied by them. If the training gear isn't good enough then players suffer. It might not sound like much, but all the little things add up to make the complete package. If the little things aren't right, then there is a fair chance the really important things won't be either.

I mean, you just have to look at the Czech Republic. When we played them in the 2002 qualifier they had the best of Puma gear on. We, on the other hand, had been wearing the same kit for about four or five years. It made us feel inferior. We asked the people in power why we were treated like second-rate citizens, but no one in our country had an answer.

On other occasions in the past we have had to cancel afternoon coaching sessions because we didn't have enough training gear, the kit from the morning session not having been washed in time. We have also encountered problems when travelling to away games. We have been made to stay in bad hotels, and there have been times when the bus that has picked us up from the airport hasn't had air-conditioning and we've ended up frying.

At other times, we would turn up for training only to find that the balls weren't blown up. We didn't have a pump so we would be forced to stop off at a petrol station and use the air pumps normally used for car tyres. It was quite embarrassing and something that a pub team shouldn't be forced to go through never mind a national side. When Roy Keane complained about the facilities that the Republic of Ireland had for their 2002 World Cup camp before heading to Japan and South Korea for the finals, I sympathised with him. I knew exactly where he was coming from.

As captain, I have the responsibility to help the players and get the best for us. I have to ask for things and do my best to make sure the players are happy and satisfied with the set-up. Most of us play for top professional clubs and are used to being treated properly every day. The standard isn't as high with the national team, and that's why it's frustrating for us.

I also have to try and make sure that the atmosphere is as good as it can be and that there is no jealousy or bickering amongst the boys. Sometimes, trying to balance all these things and prepare myself for an important match at the same time seems impossible. I really am up against it and occasionally have to fight battles with the hierarchy that I will never win – not in a million years.

It's bad enough for the players, but the real loser has to be the manager. He is the man responsible for the team's results but has had to achieve them under very difficult working conditions. A manager's preparations shouldn't be disrupted by trivial problems with training gear or flat balls. It is extremely annoying and upsets the flow of the short time that he has to get his team ready for the rigours of an international game.

Another negative side of playing for Bulgaria is that the organisation of my travel arrangements sometimes hadn't been as smooth as it should have been. A couple of years ago, I needed a visa to travel to just about anywhere in the world, and it was awkward for me when I was making my way from Scotland on my own, while most of the Bulgarian players arrived as a unit. Thankfully, the world is changing and travel restrictions have eased; I now only need a visa for countries such as America, Canada and Switzerland.

I remember leaving a Celtic winter training camp in January 2000 to go from Florida to Jamaica via Mexico to meet up with the national team for a competition. I needed a visa to get there but one wasn't organised and I had to fly from there to London to pick up a visa and then board a plane back across the Atlantic to Jamaica. It meant I had to travel for more than a full day when the journey should only have been a few hours. It was a farcical situation and unfair on my mind and body.

You've no idea how jealous it makes me when I see people from other countries just flashing their passports to enter the country of their destination. Hopefully, I will have a British passport before too long, as I now qualify for one, having lived in the UK for the required period.

Despite all the difficulties in playing for Bulgaria, it's important to just get on with it. I have found out there's no point in moaning about things. All you can do is try your best to put things right, and if your efforts aren't appreciated, you just have to stand aside and get on with the football. I know I'm not the only footballer who feels that his respective national set-up could be better.

All I want is to have a happy and successful time with the national team and make the country proud of us again. It's going to be a long and difficult process, but our goals are achievable. Reaching the 2004 European finals was a good start, but we have to build on that success.

I'm very proud to be captain of my country, and it's my dream to lead us to the World Cup finals. I hope we get there one day, and I know it's a huge ambition for our new coach, Hristo Stoichkov. He is a decent man and has some good ideas. He is also a perfectionist and demands a high level of professionalism. If we can get things right off the pitch, we will be not too far from success on it. He will want to make his mark right away by leading us to success.

The last thing I want is to go through my entire career without making it to the World Cup finals with my country. I've been jealous in the past when the likes of Henrik Larsson and Johan Mjällby have gone to major championships. It must be an incredible feeling and an absolute honour to take part in such memorable occasions on a regular basis. In fact, I'd go as far as to say that a player, no matter what he has achieved at club level, does not feel like an absolute success unless he has been to the World Cup finals with his country. South Africa in 2010 might be my best chance as we will not be at the 2006 World Cup finals in Germany.

13

My Favourite Games

I consider myself lucky to have played so many exciting and memorable games in my career when I have only been a professional for a relatively short time. I'd like to think I've many more years left at a high level and in that time I'd hope to add a few more games to the list of those that will stay in my mind forever.

When I sat down to think about all the matches that I've played, I must admit that I found it difficult narrowing my favourite matches down to five because there are dozens that come to mind without having to think too hard. However, I have managed to select a list of eight games from my career that really stand out.

BULGARIA v. ENGLAND 9 June 1999
My first choice has to be the game that made possible everything that I have now. It was a Euro 2000 qualifier and the night that Celtic decided to make their move after keeping tabs on me for a few weeks. I played in midfield and felt that I showed up well against Jamie Redknapp and David Batty. Thank goodness I did do well, because if I had flopped that night Celtic might well have

turned to another player, and I might not have a career to justify the writing of this book.

Kevin Keegan was in charge of England at the time, and they performed not too badly, although I got the feeling that they expected to turn up at our place and win by three or four goals. We had Martin Petrov sent off after an hour, and Keegan's side still couldn't take advantage. England took the lead on 15 minutes when Alan Shearer scored from six or seven yards out, but we equalized three minutes later when Georgi Markov scored with a header from Hristo Stoichkov's cross.

The game was all about Stoichkov. It was his final appearance for Bulgaria, and he made a point of going round all the young players after the game to tell them that they were the future of our country. He said that it was up to them to make everyone in Bulgaria proud of their national team. To be honest, despite Stoichkov's words of encouragement, we were all a bit down because he was the man we looked to in every game for inspiration, and we felt we were more or less doomed without him.

Now that I'm captain I haven't forgotten Stoichkov's words. I feel I owe it to him to make him proud of the Bulgarian team. We want to put the last few years of failure behind us and make Bulgaria a respected nation in the world of football once again. I am honoured to be the captain and honoured to have followed in the footsteps of Stoichkov. Two or three years from now, I want the young players in the national team to look to me for that something extra, the way I used to look to Hristo.

CELTIC v. RANGERS 27 August 2000

I don't suppose that I'll need to remind any Celtic fans of the final score of my second choice, and I'm sure the 6–2 win will top a few of their favourite game lists. Rangers had dominated the derby fixture for about a decade and must have won at least 75 per cent of the clashes. However, that afternoon the tide changed.

It was Martin O'Neill's first Old Firm game in charge, and what a start it was for the new Celtic boss. We were a goal up inside 90 seconds when Chris Sutton won the break of the ball from a corner kick and slammed it in from close range. After seven minutes, I managed to get on the score sheet when I made a run away from Fernando Ricksen to get on the end of Lubo Moravcik's corner and head home. Lubo then set up Paul Lambert in the 11th minute and he drilled a shot from the edge of the penalty box past Stefan Klos. I remember asking the dugout how long had gone in the game and they replied that it was only 15 minutes. Just 15 minutes? We were already three up. It really was incredible stuff.

Rangers came back at us when Claudio Reyna scored just before half-time. We were a little bit worried because fight backs can happen in Old Firm games, but the manager got a hold of us at half-time and calmed us down. He told us that we were doing brilliantly, but he wanted the three-goal lead restored as soon as possible. The manager's wish came true a few minutes into the second half when Henrik Larsson scored as good an individual goal as I've ever seen. Chris Sutton met Jonathan Gould's clearance, and he flicked the ball into Henrik's path. He nutmegged Bert Konterman and then raced away from Lorenzo Amoruso before beautifully chipping the ball over the head of Klos from 22 yards out into the empty net.

Rangers were back in it for a moment when Billy Dodds scored a penalty but we hit back, and Henrik made it 5–2 when he headed home a free-kick. Barry Ferguson was then red carded, and Sutton scored his second of the afternoon right on the final whistle, sliding to get on the end of Stéphane Mahé's low cross.

No one was a failure that day, and every one of us played a significant part, but I feel obliged to single out Bobby Petta for his outstanding performance. He terrorised Ricksen down the left-hand side with skill and pace. Fernando was suffering so badly Rangers manager Dick Advocaat took him off after only 25 minutes.

After the game, our dressing-room was one big party zone. We were so happy because Rangers had made us suffer for a while, and it was sweet to finally taste victory against them. We never looked back from that 90 minutes and went on to win the league and cup Double. The club brought out a video afterwards called the *Demolition Derby*, and I have to confess that I bought a few copies. I was so proud to play for Celtic in that game, and I still love to stay at home on a quiet evening with Paulina and relive the magic of that famous game.

CELTIC v. BARCELONA 11 March 2004

We'd beaten FK Teplice from the Czech Republic to set up a clash with one of the most famous clubs in world football and knew that the winners of the tie would play in the quarter-finals against the team that progressed from the Roma v. Villarreal clash.

Now, despite having reached the UEFA Cup final the season before, we were written off, most people expecting us to lose heavily to Barca. To be fair to the Catalan club, they played some incredible stuff in the first half and had a couple of clear-cut chances to open the scoring. Ronaldinho was in magnificent form, and it was an educational experience to be on the same pitch as him that night.

The game took a dramatic twist during the half-time break when the German referee, Wolfgang Stark, sent off Rab Douglas and Barca's Thiago Motta. I didn't see anything happen in the tunnel, but the referee insisted there was an incident. I think the police ended up involved for a moment or two to calm things down, and the ref came into our dressing-room during the break to send off big Rab. It meant we had to put young David Marshall in goal – a name everyone is familiar with now but one that was largely unheard of at that time. He was nervous, but the manager, players and former goalkeeping coach Terry Gennoe all assured him he had nothing to fear. David played really, really well and was even confident enough to chip the ball over the head of one of the Barca players when he was dealing with a back pass.

Despite Barca's domination of the possession and brilliance on the ball, we stunned everyone by winning the game. Javier Saviola was red carded on 49 minutes when he had a kick at Alan

Thompson, and we made the one-man advantage count with the only goal of the tie. I crossed from out on the right and found Henrik Larsson inside the box. The excellent Carlos Puyol had handled Henrik well all night but lost him for that split second, and Henrik made him pay. He headed the ball into the path of Thommo, who adjusted well to get his left leg up and over the ball to volley it into the net from six yards past Victor Valdés.

Barca were stunned, and, to be honest, I was as well. When I go into every game I genuinely believe that we can win, but that was a night when you know that on paper the odds are heavily stacked against you. Despite the difficulty of the task, we battled and worked for each other and never gave them a minute's peace.

Frank Rijkaard had not long taken over Barca and was doing well. That season, he eventually took them from near the bottom of the table to finish just a few points off the top. It showed the level that we had to hit that night and in the next match. We were expected to be on the receiving end of a hammering in Barcelona in the second leg but put in an incredible defensive shift to secure a 0–0 draw. Everyone played well that night, but young David Marshall was particularly impressive and pulled off at least two stunning saves to take us through.

CELTIC v. DUNFERMLINE 22 May 2004

My fourth choice is when we beat the Pars 3–1 at Hampden and is memorable for so many reasons. Of course, it was Henrik's last game, and we all wanted to make sure he left on as big a high as possible. He made sure of that himself when he scored two great goals. It was never going to be an easy game, and we knew Jimmy Calderwood would have his players well organised, prepared to attack and generally up for it. They took the lead with a debatable goal when David Marshall, under pressure from Derek Young, looked to have been fouled as he jumped to collect an Andrius Skerla header, but Stuart Dougal, the referee that day, waved play on and the goal stood.

Shocks happen in finals, and we were determined not to be on the end of one that afternoon. Henrik stepped it up a gear after the break and scored two spectacular goals to put us ahead. A one-goal lead is always dangerous, but I scored our third to give us that extra cushion. It took the game away from Dunfermline; they were always going to struggle to score twice against us.

At the final whistle, I was really pleased for Henrik, who scored his 242nd and final goal for Celtic that day, and for the rest of the guys. I was equally happy for myself because it was the first time that I'd won the Scottish Cup, and it meant that I had completed the full set of medals in Scotland.

I felt like I had played well that day. I know that first and foremost it's about the team's success, but playing well as an individual always makes you a little bit happier. Beating Dunfermline also helped to make up for missing out on the 2001 final win over Hibs, after I was sidelined with a broken leg, and losing the 2002 final to Rangers, after they scored an injury-time winner to make it 3–2. Our Cup triumph set me off in a really good mood for the European Championship finals in Portugal with Bulgaria that summer.

CELTIC v. JUVENTUS 31 October 2001

We turned in an amazing performance to beat the Italian champions that night, but it still wasn't enough to take us through to the next group stage of the Champions League, and we were left with mixed emotions. It was a real ding-dong match, and everyone inside a packed Celtic Park was treated to a night that they'll never forget.

Juve took the lead when Alessandro Del Piero scored a wonder goal direct from a free-kick from 22 yards out. Some people perhaps expected the roof to cave in but we recovered well. We equalized when Lubo Moravcik sent over a cross that found the head of Joos Valgaeren and he buried the ball in the back of the net. Chris Sutton was in unbelievable form that night and put us ahead just before half-time when he climbed above his marker to head home. I was a substitute, and when that goal went in I can honestly say that I have never heard noise like it at a football match. I think the atmosphere our fans created that night was even better than in the 6–2 Old Firm game. They really drove us on in that game and were rewarded with a special performance from Lubo. His display was as good as you'll ever see by any footballer. He teased and tormented the Italians and even nutmegged them on occasion. It was his final Champions League game, and for the 65 minutcs that he graced the pitch he was world class. The way he exchanged the ball all night from one foot to the other was breathtaking and showed that to be a top footballer you have to have two good feet. He gave everyone a lesson on how football should be played. God, I miss him.

I actually came on for Lubo in that game, and by that time the score was 4–2 in our favour. David Trezeguet had equalized for Juve after 50 minutes with a powerful shot, but Henrik had put us back into the lead from the penalty spot. Then Chris Sutton scored a fantastic goal with a volley from 18 yards – he was so unlucky not to get a hat-trick that night. The Italians made it 4–3 near the end when Trezeguet scored again, but we managed to hold on for the win.

It was a great result and offered us a wee bit of revenge after they had conned their way to victory a month earlier in Turin. However, we desperately wanted qualification to go with it. Unfortunately, Porto managed to get the result they wanted against Rosenborg to take them through. Martin O'Neill told us in the dressing-room after the game that we should be proud of ourselves and to walk around with our heads held high.

The Champions League campaign that season was a tremendous experience. We'll never forget it, and it has made the players hungry to repeat it as often as we can.

ANDORRA v. BULGARIA 10 September 2003

Bulgaria beat Andorra 3–0 in September 2003 with a goal from Dimitar Berbatov and a Marian Hristov double, and it secured our qualification for Euro 2004 in Portugal as group winners. It was a tough section, and to win the automatic qualification place ahead of Croatia and Belgium was a huge achievement.

It was the first time that the country had made it to major finals since Euro 96 in England, and the whole country was ecstatic. We were headline news for days and days. Television, radio and the newspapers couldn't get enough of us and we were constantly asked to give interviews. It was a really good feeling because the people of Bulgaria had been depressed about the state of their national game in the years since the exploits of the great 1994 side. Qualification gave everyone in the country interested in football a lift. The team finally had some belief in itself; it had been a long time coming. There is no substitute for the feel-good factor of qualifying for a major tournament.

RANGERS v. CELTIC 29 April 2001

Believe it or not, my seventh choice of favourite game is one I didn't even play in! I was stuck at home recovering from my broken leg and had my mattress on the floor of the living room to lie back with Paulina to watch the game.

Not for the first time that season we absolutely roasted Rangers, and it made for great television viewing, although I would have preferred to have been playing. It was the fourth-last league game of the season, and we had already wrapped up the title. It was a day for celebration and an attempt to widen the gap at the top of the table from 18 to 21 points.

It was 0–0 at half-time, but we could have been a goal down had Rod Wallace not squandered a great chance for them. We took control in the second half, and, once again, it was that man Moravcik who stole the show. He produced two moments of genius to score two goals against Stefan Klos. Watching on TV, I could see just how happy Lubo was with his afternoon's work, and he must have wished he was 25 instead of 35.

By that time Rangers were dying for the final whistle, but we looked as though we could have played on for a month! Henrik rounded off an excellent day's work when he scored three minutes from the end. The boys celebrated to the full and took a bow in front of our happy fans in the Broomloan Road stand as they lapped up every single second of the victory on that beautiful sunny day. I have to admit to having a tear in my eye as I watched it all. I felt really emotional because I knew how good the lads were feeling, and I was a little frustrated at being stuck in the house with a broken leg, unable to contribute.

The other plus point for Celtic that day was the introduction of Shaun Maloney to first-team football. He came on with 20 minutes left and even had a chance to score. He didn't manage a goal that day, but he's scored plenty since and has a bright future in football. He is now looking sharp again after recovering from a horrific cruciate-ligament knee injury. I think that Shaun is one of a number of kids at Parkhead who can go all the way in the game.

When I first came to Celtic we had a good batch of young players, including Colin Healy, Stephen Crainey and Jamie Smith. They have all left now, and I was sorry to see them leave without really stamping their full potential on the football club. I often shared a room with Colin when we were on trips, and he was a great lad – very quiet but good company. He often told me about how frustrated he was at not playing more regularly. He has a great brain for the game and can read it well. He is calm and composed and would be an asset to any side. He was very unfortunate not to go to the 2002 World Cup finals with the Republic of Ireland but will get there one day and make a real impact.

Stephen Crainey has a lovely left foot – a rare thing these days – and can hit accurate passes from 50 or 60 yards for fun. He's already been capped for Scotland and is highly rated. I thought he had the ability to go on and become a regular in the Celtic team for the next ten years, but he chose to leave and is now at Leeds United after a short spell with Southampton.

Jamie Smith is another young player with a lot of talent. He can operate down either wing and works very hard on improving both feet. He should go on to make a real name for himself, and after doing well in a short spell in the Netherlands with Den Haag, he's now back in Scotland with Aberdeen.

There's no doubt it's difficult for youngsters to make the grade at Celtic, but we have another batch on the way: guys like Aiden McGeady, David Marshall, John Kennedy, Craig Beattie, Ross Wallace and Stephen McManus. I hope all of those boys go on to do well for Celtic. With money a bit tighter in the game nowadays, they will have a real chance of becoming first-team regulars. The senior players and management around them want to help them all to progress, and that should stand them in good stead. If it doesn't work out for all of them, they have the ability to make it elsewhere at a high level. But I hope they are here, and I am here with them, for a few years yet.

ST JOHNSTONE v. CELTIC 14 March 2001

The eighth and final selection on my list might take you by surprise because it's the game in which I broke my leg in Perth. Maybe it's a weird choice as one my favourites, but I have my reasons. Of course, I didn't go out that night for the re-arranged match – after fog caused the original match to be called off – with the intention of breaking my leg, and I'm gutted that it happened. However, that game taught me a lesson that I'll remember for the rest of my career. The way I see it is that I was so unlucky to break my leg, but it could have been much, much worse. My career could have ended that night, and I was given a serious warning. Breaking my leg in that fashion has taught me never to go for a hopeless cause any more. Silly tackles are exactly that – silly. I made one that night when I slid in on Jim Weir, and I was never going to get the ball. I won't make the same mistake again. Apart from the fact that I believe that I may have cursed myself by breaking my routine that night, I also have to take much of the blame for what happened.

I feel that I have improved as a footballer over the past two and half years since breaking my leg. My touch is better, my left foot has really improved, my fitness and positional awareness are much better, the timing of my runs into the box has been enhanced and I'm also happy with the goals that I now contribute to the team. In saying that, I still have a long way to go – a very long way. I often wonder what stage I'd be at just now if the leg break hadn't happened. I get angry with myself when I think about it because I feel I'd be a better player just now, and I know that it could have been avoided.

That night was going so well up until the 82nd minute when I broke my leg. We were on our way to the title, and it was just a case of being professional in our approach to each game. We took the lead in the first half when Tommy Johnson tucked away Alan Thompson's cross, but St Johnstone equalized with a Stuart McCluskey header before the interval. We hit back, and on the 61-minute mark Alan Thompson provided another fine cross that Henrik Larsson managed to get on the end of. The game was won, and we were on our way to the title, but it wasn't a night of celebration for me. Still, I always try to take a positive out of a negative situation, and that's why this game is one that I'll never forget.

14

My Fantasy XI

I'm always interested in reading and hearing about the stars that other players admire so I've put together a dream team of guys that I'd love to have played with. As manager of my Fantasy XI, I'd set out a 3-5-2 formation because it is the one I am used to, and it is as effective a system as you'll get.

In goal I'd have to go for the colourful character **Oliver Kahn**. He has been the most consistent keeper in Europe for the past six or seven years, although I accept that his best days may now be behind him as he comes towards the end of his playing career at the highest level.

He is known in the game to be a perfectionist, but that just helps him to reach his high standards week in, week out. Kahn is excellent in one-on-one situations and is also a really good organiser. We played against Bayern Munich in the 2003–04 Champions League campaign, and he was different class in both matches. He managed to pull off a couple of great saves at vital times. We took only one point from both games, but I'm certain that if he wasn't in goal we would have won at least one of those.

You Can Call Me Stan

Like every player he has had his depressing moments in football and will feel aggrieved that he didn't win the 2002 World Cup final with Germany when they lost 2–0 to Brazil, especially as he was at fault for the first goal. He has won the European Cup and the UEFA Cup, though. Kahn has had a wonderful career, and managers throughout Europe would have loved to have had him in their side.

Consistent, quality keepers are so hard to find, and Kahn will be a tough act to follow when he hangs up his gloves. Future keepers of Bayern and Germany will always be compared with him.

My right-sided centre-back is **Johan Mjällby**. Let me make it clear, I'm not picking Johan because he used to be my teammate at Celtic. He's in my side because he is an outstanding defender and has performed well in the World Cup and European Championships. I also like guys at the back that don't try any fancy stuff or things that they can't do. Johan is the type of guy I would trust with my football life. He is honest, brave and never shirks out of a 50/50 challenge. His sheer physical presence has frightened the life out of so many opponents, but he is not a dirty player – he is fair.

It took him a while to get into Martin O'Neill's first team, but once he got his chance, he became a permanent fixture. Johan is also a good man to have in the dressing-room and was excellent for team morale at Parkhead. Players respected and looked up to him, and it takes a strong character to reach that level.

I was sad to see him leave Celtic in the summer of 2004. Of course, I understood his reasons. Levante made him a good offer and he grabbed it. His wife and children love life on the outskirts of Valencia, with sunshine on their backs most of the year. I reckon Johan will go into management in the future, and I think he has the qualities to be a success as a gaffer.

In the centre of the back three I can't ignore the Brazilian **Lucio**. My international teammate Dmitar Berbatov used to play with him at Bayer Leverkusen and raved about him. Lucio is strong in the air and strong in the tackle, but he can also play football. He often brings the ball out from the back to set up attacks for his team. I'm told that he's even competitive in training and hates losing a five-a-side game or any of the sprints.

Any time I have watched him I have been impressed, and there aren't many better than him at this moment. He proved his worth by helping Brazil win the World Cup in 2002.

He's now playing for Bayern Munich and has been a tremendous signing for them. He has steadied their defence and is a player they will be desperate to hang on to.

To complete my back line I'd choose England's **Rio Ferdinand**. Rio has been superb for the past three seasons and must be the most improved defender in the world during that time. He now has a presence on the pitch and a reputation that makes strikers apprehensive about facing him. Rio's growth in the game has been a good one, going from West Ham to Leeds and then to Manchester United. A lot has been made of the fact that Sir Alex Ferguson paid the best part of £30 million for him, but I believe he will prove to be worth every single penny over the course of his Old Trafford career.

Obviously, he suffered a major setback in the early part of 2004 when he was banned from playing football after failing to turn up for an English FA drugs test. The whole world had an opinion on the reasons behind his non-appearance, and the non-stop intrusion into his private life at that time must have been so difficult to deal with. At the end of the day, he has served his time, and his life has moved on. I'm told his attitude during his time out was superb, even though he had to miss going to Portugal with England for the 2004 European Championship finals because of the ban. When Rio's ban was over, Ferguson put him straight back in against Liverpool at Old Trafford, and he was immense that night against difficult opponents with the eyes of the football world focused on his every move for the whole 90 minutes.

He never looks uncomfortable in any situation, and his coolness, as well as his undoubted ability, rubs off on those around him. For sure, he'd be in any team that I was in charge of or playing in.

I was tempted to go for David Beckham on the right-hand side of midfield, but, for me, **Luís Figo** is a much more accomplished player. He has played at the highest level for Barcelona, Real Madrid and now Inter and managed to cope with the pressures of being at such high-profile clubs. Figo is a fine player down the right but is also a natural at coming inside with the ball and opening up the middle of the park. The fact that he is so unpredictable with the ball at his feet gives him the edge over any other contenders for the right midfield slot.

It's amazing to think that Barcelona managed to get him for less than £2 million in 1995 from Sporting Lisbon and then made a profit of around £35 million five years later when they sold him to Real. Great business, but I'm sure that they would have preferred to keep him, which tells you plenty about his class. He has had to go through some uncertain times at Real, as they seem to chop and change their head coach every five minutes. Many players have had their say on the situation and have criticised the club, but Figo has kept his thoughts to himself to show that, apart from being a fine footballer, he is also a good person.

The first central-midfield place has to go to **Patrick Vieira**. Vieira is a player that every coach in the world would love to have, and every big club from Manchester United to Chelsea and Real Madrid tried to buy him from Arsenal but all failed for a variety of reasons. Eventually, Arsène Wenger relented this summer when Patrick was sold to Juventus. He may have felt that the midfielder was just past his peak, and who can argue with Wenger's judgement? But, in my opinion, Patrick is strong, has pace and boasts an intimidating presence on the pitch. He also gives excellent protection to the back line and works tirelessly in every other area of the pitch, contributing goals at important times.

His temperament has been called into question over the past few seasons as he has picked up a few red cards, but I don't think there is any real malice in his play. The only things that he is guilty of are an insatiable desire for success and a hatred of losing. When he was missing from the Arsenal side there's no doubt that they suffered as a result. Yes, they have talent all over the pitch and flair players such as Robert Pires, Thierry Henry and Cesc Fàbregas, but the heartbeat of the team came from Vieira.

Alongside him I'd have two attacking midfielders as I believe with the strength and experience of the defenders and Vieira they'd cover the team well when the opposition attacked. Rivaldo was in my thoughts because he's been a consistent performer at the highest level for four or five years and has won a World Player of the Year award as a reward for his successes. He was also a major contributor to Brazil's 2002 World Cup victory. His first touch is impeccable, and he's the type of player I'd pay to watch. However, I've decided to go for my countryman **Krassimir Balakov**. He is one of the finest footballers to have played for Bulgaria and is adored by everyone in the country. It was a pleasure to play alongside him for the national team. He has tremendous vision and had a wonderful ability to ghost into great goal-scoring positions. He was also a tremendous influence in our dressing-room and had the ability to remain calm when all around people were nervous or anxious. That kind of temperament is vital, particularly if you need to pull things together at half-time because you are behind in the game or things are just not going to plan. He is now on the coaching staff at Stuttgart, and they value him so highly after his contribution there as a player that he probably has a job for life if he wants it.

I thought about Zinedine Zidane to fill the final central-midfield position, but I'm not as big a fan of his as some others are. You might think that I'm off my head to ignore him and the likes of Ronaldinho, but I believe **Michael Ballack** is a much better bet for the other attacking midfield role. Ballack was so unfortunate to be ruled out of the 2002 World Cup final because of suspension. I thought that he had a fantastic tournament and Germany would have stood a much better chance if he had been available. I played against him in a friendly for Bulgaria, and he was very impressive. He also played for Bayern against us in the Champions League after he moved there from Bayer Leverkusen on a Bosman transfer following the 2002 Champions League final at Hampden.

Ballack is the kind of player that I can learn from and the kind of talent that I strive to become. He's still very young, and his move to Bayern will improve him as a player. Within the next two years, I expect him to become a world-famous name, and every major club across Europe will be willing to spend bucketloads of cash to land him.

On the left-hand side in the wing-back role there's only one option for me and that's the great **Roberto Carlos**. The Brazilian never seems to be injured and has the energy and ability to operate up and down the side of the pitch all day. He is also capable of scoring from set pieces – or anywhere within 45 yards of goal! You can see goalkeepers visibly nervous every time he has the ball within shooting range. I always enjoy watching him in action, and it's a thrill to watch him deliver corners and free-kicks into the box. He is so accurate, and it really is an ambition of mine to play in the same team as him one day. I'd love to see how he prepares for a game, how he motivates himself and how he reacts to a win or a defeat. So Roberto, if you ever fancy coming to play for Celtic, I'm sure that the club would love to see you as much as I would!

Up front, I have so many great players to choose from: Thierry Henry, Andriy Shevchenko, Wayne Rooney, the list seems endless. Ronaldo was heavily in my thoughts as he can score a goal against any opposition at any given time. After the problems he had at France 98, I was pleased to see him finish top scorer in the World Cup four years later. But I'm going to ignore the Brazilian and make a brave decision, as all managers have to do. I think there is a saying that goes along the lines of 'If you're afraid of making a decision, you'll never decide on anything', so I'm going for **Hristo Stoichkov**. I can hear you accusing me of selecting another fellow countryman, but Stoichkov was the best in the business when he was at the peak of his playing career for Barcelona and Bulgaria. He was voted the European Footballer of the Year in 1995, and no one could argue with that decision.

Hristo had a nose for goal, and some of the strikes he came up with were absolutely spectacular. His movement was always clever, and he created so much space and so many scoring opportunities for his strike partners over the years. He's the biggest star to have come out of Bulgaria, and it's a pity that he isn't still around to play for the national team.

I was fortunate to have played with Hristo during his international career and towards the end of his club career when he came back home to play for CSKA Sofia. He was the type of player that made it look like anything was possible when he had the ball at his feet. He's now in charge of the Bulgarian national team, and I'm sure he will do well in the job.

The final place in my side, to partner Stoichkov, has to go to **Henrik Larsson**. Henrik will be embarrassed about me choosing him ahead of the likes of Michael Owen and Ruud van Nistelrooy, and, again, I'll probably be accused of only picking him because he played with me at Celtic, but that's not the case. Henrik has been a quality player for many years and managed to win Europe's Golden Boot in 2001 – the season after he broke his leg – when he bagged 53 goals. He's on a par with any striker in the world. Apart from his ability on the pitch, he is also a credit off it as he always conducts himself properly and professionally. He is a natural goal scorer and is the same in training as he is on the pitch on a Saturday – absolutely lethal. That's why he gets my vote.

I just wish I was still able to witness his prowess at first hand, but, sadly for Celtic, he's now with Barcelona. I know that he will do well there and will be remembered fondly by the Barca fans once his career comes to an end. He was unlucky with a bad knee injury in his first season, but when he's fit, the Nou Camp will provide the perfect platform for his undoubted talents.

The coach of my fantasy team would be **Johan Cruyff**, who is one of the greatest players ever to grace the game. I've never met him but I'd dearly love to. My admiration for Johan stems from conversations I've had with Hristo Stoichkov. Hristo played for him at Barcelona and told me that he is a man, and a manager, that players responded to and loved. He treated them like adults off the pitch and allowed them to express themselves on it, albeit with the proper guidance. I'm also told that he has a great sense of humour. In many ways he sounds too good to be true – apart from the fact that he smoked about 100 cigarettes a day! I can't remember him too well from his playing days, but his record speaks for itself, winning the European Footballer of the Year award in 1971, 1972 and 1973.

There's a theory that most great players don't make great managers, but Johan blew that apart when he took Barcelona to four league championships and the European Cup. One of the very best, and a brilliant leader for my team.

15

72 Hours in My Life

It is important for a footballer to look after himself as best he can throughout the whole season in order to keep his mind and body in tip-top condition. It is also vital to make sure that a footballer properly prepares himself in the build-up to the match and conducts himself in the correct manner on the day after the 90 minutes.

With this in mind, I will try and give you an insight into a typical 72 hours in my life, including the lead-up to a game on the Saturday, the big day itself and the day after. This routine is how I would normally prepare myself mentally and physically for a typical match. The weekend that I have chosen to illustrate what it is like to be me is the one when I played against Motherwell at Celtic Park on 23 January 2005. We won the match 2–0. I scored our first goal and was given the Carling Man of the Match award. I hope you believe me when I say that my good performance wasn't the reason for choosing that game: I picked it in advance – honestly! Even if I had played badly and was subbed at half-time by the gaffer, I would still have stuck with this hour and a half!

You Can Call Me Stan

The day before the game, I woke up about 8.30 a.m. after a good nine-hour sleep and got myself ready. I rarely eat breakfast in the house and decided instead to have a cup of coffee when I arrived at Celtic Park at about 9.30 a.m. I then did a set of four four-minute runs on the treadmill in the club gym, and it felt good to blow away any cobwebs from the night before.

The training session at Barrowfield was quite short and sharp, the way it is at every club in the world the day before a game. We warmed up for about fifteen minutes, did some stretching exercises and then played three seven-minute full-scale games – the young players against the old. Thankfully, I'm still in the 'young team'! We then ran through one or two things with a view to the Motherwell game.

At the end of training on a Friday we always gave out the yellow jersey to the player who had had a nightmare day. Henri Camara, Paul Lambert and Stephen McManus were all pretty close in the voting, but, in the end, it was given to McManus. I think that the yellow jersey ritual was good fun, and I'm proud to say that I only wore the dreaded top once in all the time that Martin O'Neill was at the club. It was a good laugh, and the player who won it was known as 'The Donkey of the Week'. Previously, the guy who won it would have to put it on for the whole of the following week, but we later changed it so that they just had to wear it the following Friday.

After training, I had a shower and then headed up to the players' dining room to have lunch with Stan Varga and Juninho. I chose to have pasta. I prefer eating plain pasta in the build-up to a match; I don't like a bolognese sauce – despite it being my favourite – or anything like that through it. Big Stan also had pasta and Juninho had boiled eggs! Some of the other guys like to eat beans on toast, but there's plenty of choice for whatever we feel like.

Some of the boys like to put on a fixed-odds coupon for the weekend and sit together during lunch trying to predict the outcome of the games in the English Premiership and some of the games in Scotland. I have only put a coupon on two or three times: it's not really my kind of thing.

72 Hours in My Life

The media arrive at Celtic Park on a Friday and sometimes you have to go and speak to them. I don't mind doing radio, television and newspaper stuff, but I didn't have to on that day, and it was left to Ulrik Laursen and Stephen McManus.

So, as soon as I had finished my lunch I headed outside the stadium, signed a few autographs and then got straight into my car to make my way home, arriving at about 1.30 p.m. I like to make the most of the few hours that I have with Paulina and young Stiliyan in the afternoon before a game, because we're packed off to our hotel on the Friday night to ensure that we all get proper rest and do not get disturbed.

I had a coffee with Paulina and played about the living room with Stiliyan. He has a lot of energy at the moment and enjoys running about and kicking the ball. He has started to make the connection between football and me, and it looks as if he is going to grow up with a passion for the game. However, I would never force him into getting involved in football. He will do what he wants and will receive 100 per cent backing from Paulina and me.

I left the house at 6.30 p.m. and headed to the Hilton in Glasgow city centre. We stay there on the eve of every home game and I have a room to myself in the hotel. It is good to get that kind of privacy. I like to lie in my bed at night and go through the game we will be playing the next day. I think of the opponents and then the individuals that I might be up against. I knew that Motherwell had some good young players and had been impressed with their left-back Stevie Hammell and Australian striker Scott McDonald – although I've gone off Scott in the last few months!

The squad had dinner at the hotel at about 7 p.m., and, once again, it was just plain pasta and still water with ice for me. After dinner, I went upstairs to one of our medical rooms and had a 45-minute massage. I really enjoy getting my legs massaged as I think it is vital to make sure that the muscles in your legs are totally relaxed going into a match. I sometimes take a back massage, but it just depends on the part of my body that is feeling tight. A lot of the boys like a massage before a game, and it is always good fun in there. It can be a bit chaotic when big Johnny Hartson and Chris Sutton are present. There is never a dull moment as the jokes fly back and forth across the room.

I was back in my room for about nine o'clock and sat back and watched a DVD. I have a varied taste in movies – from action to comedy to thrillers. I admire Brad Pitt and thought that he was excellent in *Seven* and more recently in *Ocean's 11*. I think that is a great movie. I also think that Robert de Niro is a brilliant actor. His performance in *Heat* with Al Pacino was exceptional, and I also thought that he played a great part in *Meet the Parents* with Ben Stiller. For him to go from playing the tough guy who has the audience on the edge of their seats to then having them laughing at him in a comedy shows his undoubted talent.

When I'd finished watching *Ocean's 11*, I read a book for a while. I enjoy reading about criminal activity and books on the presidents of the USA. They have such a powerful job, and I'm always interested to discover as much as I can about them: what makes them tick, what motivates them and how they make important, life-changing decisions. I'm also fascinated by the planning and organisation that goes into making sure a president's security arrangements are up to scratch.

I had an alarm call just after 9 a.m. on the Saturday morning and lay in bed for a while longer. I was up and about by 10 a.m. but didn't really bother with breakfast. I had some coffee and still water instead. At 11 a.m., the entire squad took a walk and headed into town for 15 minutes. After being in the hotel all night, it's good to get out and about and take in some fresh air – even if it is freezing cold air! We had our pre-match meal at 11.30 a.m., and, once again, I just had plain pasta. It may sound boring eating pasta all the time, but it's important to build up your carbohydrates and energy levels before a game. I have pasta so often on the day of a game and the day before that you can understand why I try to avoid it at all other times!

I was back in my room just before noon and watched a bit of Sky Sports. I think their coverage of the game is different class, and I sometimes wonder where football would be without it. They have fantastic programmes, great ideas and their guests are all so enthusiastic with sensible opinions and a detailed knowledge of the game.

We got on the bus at 1.10 p.m. to make our way to Celtic Park. Sometimes we have music on the bus, or we might watch a film, but at other times, the guys just have a laugh and a chat as we head to the east end of Glasgow. The journey takes about 20 minutes, and Jackie McNamara would be in charge of the pre-match entertainment! He often brought videos with him, and we would all enjoy watching Ricky Gervais in *The Office* or David Jason in *Only Fools and Horses*. Playing cards is another popular pastime on the road to our away games, and I've learned a few games since I arrived here. It was a good way of allowing me to bond with my teammates and helped me to settle in when I first joined the club. I particularly enjoy playing my speciality, 'Nominations'.

Before the Motherwell game, we had a meeting with the manager in the dressing-room just before 2 p.m., and he named the team. I'm never really nervous when it comes to the time when the gaffer reads out the line-up. I always have an idea of how I've performed during the build-up to the game and know I always give it everything in training. Sometimes you can be left out for a tactical reason, or to give you a rest, but without wishing to sound cocky, I feel like I always have a good chance of playing. I've played for Celtic for a few seasons now, and the manager knows what I can bring to the team.

Martin told me that I would be starting against Motherwell and playing on the right-hand side of midfield. In the team-talk, the manager emphasised that we had to make sure we won to maintain our lead at the top over Rangers. At that point, we were three points ahead and wanted to stretch our lead to six to put pressure on our rivals who were playing away at Aberdeen the following day.

During the warm-up, I enjoy passing the ball around and doing some short and sharp sprint exercises. We then go through a shooting routine for five or six minutes, and I think it is important to hit the target. The warm-up might not seem like much but it is important – a good warm-up has you in a better frame of mind to go out and perform well.

The Motherwell game didn't start too well for us. Very little was going our way, and our passing wasn't as good as it should have been. The manager decided to change the formation a little by making one or two positional changes. I was pushed into the centre of midfield from the right, and I felt more comfortable playing there. Alan Thompson moved to the left and Aiden McGeady was switched out to the right-hand side. Those changes seemed to galvanise us, and we started to play better. The whole team looked more relaxed and confident.

Our opening goal came on the 31-minute mark, and I'm pleased to say that I scored it. Ulrik Laursen played a pass to big John and he switched the ball to Sutton. Sutty is such a clever footballer, and he noticed me making a run beyond him into the space behind the Well defence. He played it first time into my path, and I had the goal in my sights. From about 30 yards out I drove at the Motherwell rearguard, coming in from the left towards the centre of their goal. David Partridge came across to block me, but I managed to take the ball to the side of him and set myself up with a shooting opportunity. I hit the shot with my right foot from the edge of the box, and the ball squeezed past Gordon Marshall, who had managed to get a hand to it.

I was really delighted with my goal. I'm pleased every time I score, but it's a special feeling to score in front of the Celtic supporters and in front of Paulina and young Stiliyan. I just wish that I could improve my strike rate. The goal against Motherwell was my sixth of the season, and I hoped to reach double figures by the time the campaign finished. In the end, I scored 12 goals that season.

The only problem I have with scoring is that Paulina takes the mickey out of my celebrations! She reckons that I should be a bit more adventurous, but there's no way that I'm going to end up featured on *They Think It's All Over* at the part of the show when the guests try to guess what the goal celebration is all about! I've told Paulina that by the time the ball is in the net my teammates are joining me to share the moment, and I'm not interested in trying to push them out of the way to do a Robbie Keane cartwheel and forward roll or a Lomana LuaLua somersault. As much as those goal celebrations are really entertaining, they are definitely not for me.

We scored our second goal on 56 minutes, and it was a great finish from Sutton. We took possession from Motherwell, and Thompson played Sutty through with a lovely pass. Paul Quinn was hard on his heels, but Sutton managed to keep enough distance to get a clear view of goal and remained calm to shoot past Marshall with his right foot. We were 2–0 ahead at that point and were more relaxed and confident for the rest of the match. At 1–0 there is always nervousness and a fear that one slack moment can cost two precious points, but with a two-goal lead we can usually feel a bit more secure. We are always confident that if we have a two-goal advantage at Celtic Park it will be very difficult for any team to make a comeback. At half-time, the manager had emphasised this point and urged us to go and get the second goal to kill the game and not give Motherwell any encouragement to get back into it. John Robertson and Steve Walford also pointed out a few things to the players; we always appreciate their input.

After the match, the manager was happy with the result and told us that it was a great win. However, he did point out one or two things that he wasn't happy about. For example, he felt that some of us hadn't picked up runners off the ball. It is only ever constructive criticism, and it is up to the individual player to take his advice on board and make sure that the same mistakes don't happen again.

After a tough 90 minutes, I had a shower and a bath and spoke to a couple of the boys about the result. I get changed in between Stan Varga and Alan Thompson. We have lockers in the dressing-room, and I have big Stan on my left and Alan on my right. I had won the Man of the Match award that day, and after I was changed,

You Can Call Me Stan

I headed up to the Carling Suite to collect my prize – a bottle of champagne presented to me by a five-year-old Celtic fan. I shared a little joke with the young boy and asked him if he had chosen the bottle, but he said that the older people had picked the champers.

At that point, Paul Lambert popped his head round the door and joked to everyone that he couldn't believe that they'd voted me as their man of the match! I signed some autographs and posed for photos with the Carling guests, and it was a nice way to wind down after the game. Paulina was in the players' lounge, but I prefer to stay away from there after a game. It's quite a small room, and I think it is too hot and very busy. I waited outside for Paulina and phoned her to say that I was ready to go home.

On that particular Saturday night, a couple of the boys were going out for a quiet drink, but I was feeling tired and preferred just to stay at home and have a nice family dinner. Paulina made us a beautiful Bulgarian meal, and after that, we played with young Stiliyan. He was quite tired and was in bed by about 9 p.m. Paulina and I then had a chat and watched some television. I caught up with *Match of the Day* that night and enjoyed the excitement of the Birmingham v. Fulham, Manchester United v. Aston Villa and Norwich v. Middlesbrough games.

I was in bed for about half past midnight and was up by about 10 a.m. the next day. I was still feeling quite tired, but that is normal the day after a game. The players had the day off that Sunday but a lot of times we have to go in, especially if we have a midweek game. I like having a Sunday off: it has always traditionally seemed like a day to relax and spend some quality time with the family. We had some lunch together then drove into Glasgow city centre for a walk. The shops in the town are excellent, and I enjoy looking at a few stores and buying clothes. Princes Square has some high-quality shopping, and because it's indoors, it is a good place to escape the Scottish weather!

The Rangers game was on while we were out shopping, but there was no way that I could avoid finding out how they were getting on at Pittodrie – I was being sent text messages by friends, and people on the street kept me informed. It's amazing how everyone is so wrapped up in the Old Firm, and sometimes it seems to be almost impossible to switch off from it, especially when the title race is so close. Of course, I was hopeful that Rangers would drop points, but they won 2–1 and our lead was back to three again. However, Aberdeen had made Rangers fight for their victory, and that's the way it was all season in every game for the two Old Firm teams. We always have to battle for the three points, especially when we are away from home.

Paulina, Stiliyan and I arrived back home before five o'clock, and I caught up with a few phone calls I had to make. I phoned my folks back in Bulgaria to catch up with events over there. I like to keep in touch with my homeland and regularly phone to see how things are. I also had a quick look at the Sunday papers, but I'm not really one for reading them all the time. If I have time I will do it, but I don't go out of my way to read the newspapers.

Later we had our dinner, and then I watched Real Madrid beat Real Mallorca 3–1. I gave young Stiliyan a bath and had some fun splashing in the water with him. However, I had training the next day and so was in bed for about 10.30 p.m., thinking back over the weekend that had just passed. It was a successful 72 hours: I had enjoyed scoring a goal, seeing us stay top of the league and having all day on the Sunday to spend with my family.

16

You Can Call Me Stan but Not a Diver

I have a reputation of being a diver and a cheat with some people in Scotland and that upsets and angers me. I never try to use underhand tactics to gain an advantage over the opposition. I know how difficult it is for teams to get something out of a game against Celtic, without having us diving all over the place. Players from smaller clubs put their heart and soul into games, and I wouldn't like to have it on my conscience that I cost them a valuable point or bonus money because I had cheated.

Sometimes, though, it is just impossible to keep your balance if you have been tripped or nudged. It may look like I am going down easily, but I can promise you I don't. I try to keep my balance a lot of times when I know that other players would go down. Also, if I do get knocked over, I try to get back up quickly to show that there hasn't been serious contact. I have never made a blatant dive.

There is a big difference between domestic football in Bulgaria and football in Scotland. The standard is higher, the game is more physical and the tempo of a match is much, much faster over here. Those kinds of things mean that it takes a player some time to adjust. In fact, I have been so aware of what people have tagged me that I have worked really hard in the last couple of years to improve my upper-body strength in a bid to help me to keep my balance more easily.

I don't expect every football fan to understand this as looks can be deceptive, but it really upsets me when I hear commentators and ex-professionals having a go at me on television and in newspapers saying that I dived or that I am a cheat. It is way out of order to say those things, and those ex-pros should know better.

These accusations have earned me an undeserved reputation, and I get the feeling that some referees are against me before a ball is kicked. The opposition fans also like to have a go at me during a game every time I touch the ball. I remember it all coming to a head in a league game at Kilmarnock on 12 January 2002. We won 2–0, and I won a penalty for the team. I was clearly bundled to the ground by Peter Canero, and referee John Underhill was correct to award the spot-kick. But some people had doubts in their minds about the legitimacy of the penalty because I was the player who had won us the kick. Television evidence later proved that it was the right decision, but Bobby Williamson, who was in charge of Kilmarnock at that time, doubted the decision and claimed that I had dived. He then told the media in the after-match conference that I had a reputation of winning a few dodgy decisions.

I was hurt and angered by his comments, and Williamson immediately went down in my estimation. If people have doubts about my integrity, I'd rather that they approached me directly. I'd prefer to have it out face to face because I don't think that I will ever have anything to hide or be ashamed of. To be fair to Bobby, after he had watched it on television he did phone Martin O'Neill to tell him to pass on his apologies to me, as he realised that I hadn't dived. These days, I have no problem with Bobby and know things can be said in the heat of the moment after a game, especially when your team has lost.

You Can Call Me Stan but Not a Diver

I'm not sure why I now have this reputation. Maybe it is because I am a foreigner. Sadly, a lot of players from other countries have had to put up with the same accusations. It's something that I doubt I will ever be able to shake off, and the controversy even reared up again on the first game of the 2005–06 season when Gordon Marshall accused me of diving at Fir Park. Referee Mike McCurry awarded a penalty and rightly so because contact was made. Later that night, when I watched the game on Setanta, I was delighted to see that my former teammate Craig Burley backed the decision and confirmed that he thought that it should have been a penalty.

The reputation that I have managed to acquire has also had a bearing on my life off the pitch. For instance, a few times when I have been sitting at the traffic lights in my car, a man in the next car has mimed an act of diving and given me the finger – it is not nice. It is even more disturbing when I am out shopping with Paulina and young Stiliyan and people accuse me of being a 'diving bastard'. I can take the insults, but if it hurts my wife I'm not happy. I'd rather my family weren't subjected to mindless abuse and namecalling.

Fortunately, those are isolated incidents and don't happen too often. I know that as an Old Firm player living in Glasgow I am bound to come in for some extra attention, especially when I am out socialising in the city. However, most people learn to respect your privacy, and I rarely have any problems when Paulina and I go out for dinner. We go to restaurants like Il Pavone in Glasgow, and Marco and his staff look after us well. We are also given a warm welcome at the Amber Regent and the Ho Wong in Glasgow city centre.

When I am out some supporters ask for autographs, and that is fine by me. Also, when I'm out running in the Jordanhill area at night for some extra exercise I sometimes get stopped by fans – maybe I should learn to run faster! At our house in the West End there can sometimes be a knock at the front door when one of the kids from our street wants an autograph. Most of the time it is fine and I do it, but it would be nice to have complete privacy when I'm at home relaxing with my family. At least the kids don't come to the door and attack me for being a 'diver'!

When Ian McCall was the Dundee United manager he also accused me of diving to get my team a penalty in a match against his side. He ripped me to pieces in the after-match interviews. I was angry with him – really angry. Again, after he had watched it on television, he realised that I hadn't dived and that I'd clearly been brought down. He also came out and apologised via the media a few days later. It was big of him to admit that he had called it wrong, and I now have no disagreements with him.

The Aberdeen fans have also taken a dislike to me – although show me an Old Firm player that they *do* like – and some of them pelted me with snowballs as I prepared to take a corner when we played up there in December 2001. Are we supposed to just stand and accept it? It wasn't the sort of reception I would expect, and I did not appreciate the fans' childish behaviour. That day, I felt like jumping into the Pittodrie stands and having a go at a few of them, but that's exactly what they want you to do. I refused to take the bait; these so-called fans are simply not worth responding to. I don't mind the opposition supporters booing or swearing at me during a game, but I take exception to something like that. Those idiots could have had a stone, a piece of glass or a coin inside one of the snowballs.

Being labelled a cheat is new to me. When I played in Bulgaria I was never accused of that kind of thing, and it disturbs me to think that people now charge me with the crime of being a diver here in Scotland. The referees have a lot to do with it, but I don't envy the job they have to do. They don't get paid much, and their lives can become a misery if they get something wrong in a big game. I would never want to be a referee, but there are a few in this country who should strive to be more consistent. I accept that they are only human and that referees are also entitled to a mistake here and there, just like the players.

However, they are not consistent with their yellow and red cards, and, sometimes, I do get the feeling that they do not like Celtic. Many of our fans have thought for a long time that officials in Scotland have it in for the club, and there have been occasions when I have walked off at the end of a game thinking along the same lines.

I have to say that there are a few referees on the grade one list that frankly don't deserve to be in charge of schoolboy games. I know their names, but I will only end up in trouble with the authorities if I name them, and I don't want that to happen. I would exempt the likes of Hugh Dallas and Kenny Clark from that list of culprits, and I also think Mike McCurry is improving all the time. They usually get the big decisions right, and if more of their colleagues were as calm as they are and as good with their man-management on the pitch, then there wouldn't be so many problems. They treat the players like human beings and aren't afraid to explain their decisions and have a quiet word in your ear when the time is right.

Believe it or not, the occasional bit of banter is also exchanged between players and refs. Willie Young is a prime example. He is chatty on the pitch and has a sense of humour that can be helpful in taking the heat out of a nasty situation. I remember listening to his after-dinner speech at the Scottish Football Writers' Player of the Year award dinner in 2002 and thinking that he was exceptionally funny. It made me realise that referees do have a human side – despite what many fans think – and I bet many of them would actually be decent company on a night out. We have quite a bit in common with them, and I believe that getting us together for a chat, even it was just once a month at training, wouldn't be a bad thing. There shouldn't be a 'them and us' mentality. It's a pity that they feel that it isn't appropriate for them to lighten up on the pitch. I'm not asking them to run around cracking jokes, but if we had a bit more communication, the game would be much better off.

It would also help if they were all top-class referees, but, unfortunately, they're not. Just as it is in every walk of life – whether salesman, doctor or chef – some are better than others. The referees that are not at the same standard as the top ones should be held accountable for some of their decisions and eventually be suspended or demoted if they get things wrong more often than not. A strict system like that has to be introduced for the good of the game.

I do have sympathy for the referees because of the way that their games are distributed. The top refs should be handling the SPL matches at least nine games out of ten, but I have noticed that they might be in charge of an Old Firm game one week then the next refereeing at East Stirling or East Fife. And Albion Rovers or Peterhead the week after that. That's not right and doesn't do anybody any favours.

In saying that, at least over here the referees are not corrupt. In Bulgaria, it's believed that some referees take bribes. Not all of them but a few. Of course, it is hard to prove, but the Bulgarian authorities must know it goes on. I would love to think that Bulgarian football would eradicate this kind of thing in the near future, but I don't think that will be possible. The scandal and suspicion may well just be part of the game, and that is a real shame. It has ruined many good matches in the past and will ruin even more in the future.

On the positive side, the Bulgarian Football Union (BFU) are now starting to take steps to try and stamp out any corruption, and they have begun to investigate any accusations made about referees or clubs. The year that I left Bulgarian football to join Celtic, Metalurg Pernik were relegated after the BFU found them guilty of match fixing. Litex Lovech, who won the league that season, and Levski Sofia were deducted three points each for winning fixed matches against Metalurg. Referees, linesmen and fourth officials were suspended as a result and some games were forced to be replayed.

How dishonest people in football can look at themselves in the mirror, I will never know. They are spoiling what should be good games for the fans and messing with players' livelihoods, and it shouldn't be allowed to happen anywhere in the world. I feel strongly about this issue, and that is why I have emphasised here that I am not a diver or a cheat, despite what some people may think.

17

Charity Work
and Future Plans

Most of the letters that I receive at Celtic Park are from fans congratulating me on playing well or wishing the boys and me all the best for any big games that we may have coming up. Occasionally, however, a letter arrives that brings a lump to your throat and a tear to your eye.

That's precisely what happened early in 2002 when I was heartbroken to read about the situation that a young Bulgarian boy found himself in. His name was Ilyan Bakalov and he had cerebral palsy. Since birth, he had been paralysed from the waist down. He was nine when I first heard about his sad plight – God help him. The Lighthouse Trust, a cerebral palsy charity, wrote to me to explain his situation. They also explained that operations are very expensive in Bulgaria and that the standard of care leaves a lot to be desired.

As soon as I read about poor Ilyan's situation I decided to help raise £3,000 to buy him a wheelchair after his mother told me that she was worried that the standard of treatment that he was receiving in Bulgaria wasn't good enough. It was at that point that Paulina came up with the idea of raising enough money to bring him to Scotland to have him treated here.

It was a fantastic suggestion from my wife, and we decided to get in touch with our friend Milan Cvetkovc who organised a theme night with help from Harlequin Leisure Group. Harlequin offered their premises at their Indian restaurant on the south side of Glasgow and a charity night was organised for April 2002. We made it a mixed 'theme night' of Indian and Bulgarian food, and around 350 people turned up to make it a very worthwhile occasion.

I spoke to the boys at the club and everyone donated something to help raise the money. Lubo Moravcik donated his boots, and I think they fetched about £10,000. Henrik Larsson and John Hartson handed in signed jerseys, which also helped raise a significant amount of cash in the auction. The media in Scotland also helped to raise awareness of Ilyan's cause, and it's one thing that they deserve a lot of credit for. Whenever there's a story that touches the hearts of Scottish people, the media get behind it and do as much as they can to drive it on and give it the publicity it deserves. Then, the overwhelming generosity of the Scottish people takes over, and they do everything they can to find some money to help a person in need.

The night for Ilyan was a great success. A camera crew from New Television had come over from Bulgaria to film the event as part of a programme that they were making about me and what my life was like in Glasgow as a Celtic player. They couldn't believe the generosity of the Scottish people and returned to Bulgaria raving about the country. The likes of Lubo, big Johnny Hartson, Bobo Balde and Momo Sylla came along to lend their support that night, and it was much appreciated. Footballers don't often receive the credit that they deserve for doing charity work. A lot of guys do lots of work but ask for it not to be made public.

One recent event that touched every footballer's heart was the Indian Ocean earthquake and tsunami disaster in late 2004. Almost immediately after it happened, the players and staff at Celtic decided to make a financial donation to the relief fund. I know that the Rangers boys also contributed and most clubs around Britain and Europe donated a significant amount of money to help with the aftermath. I wish that there were ways of avoiding days like that one. It would be great to wave a magic wand to turn the clock back and prevent the deaths of thousands of innocent people. Mothers and fathers, brothers and sisters – so many loved ones for so many people around the world died that day, and I pray that nothing like that ever happens again.

At least with young Ilyan, we were able to try to make his day-to-day existence more comfortable. We hoped that the money we raised from the charity night would help to improve his quality of life and make him feel as comfortable as possible. I know that he has been responding well to treatment and is feeling much better these days. Improvement in these cases doesn't happen overnight and he can't be cured, but if the medical help that we were able to pay for can help him to feel even 5 per cent better, I will be so happy for him and his family.

When I think of the trivial things in life that I moan about, one thought of little Ilyan's situation hammers home just how lucky I am. However, some of the letters that I receive are not so deserving of attention as young Ilyan's was. In fact, some of the people writing to me are chancers, and it's hard for me to decide the good guys from the bad guys. Some causes are very deserving, and it only takes a few phone calls to find out if they are authentic requests. Thankfully, it takes even less time to expose the ones who are trying to con something out of you.

The letter that most sticks in my mind arrived at Celtic Park about four months after I had arrived at the club. It was from a man in my home town of Montana whom I'd never heard of before. He wrote that now that I was a millionaire after my move to Britain, it shouldn't be a problem for me to send him £100 so he could buy himself a new pair of shoes, a new shirt and a pair of trousers! Now the guy may genuinely have needed some new clothes, but I didn't think it was up to me to finance him. In any case, at that stage in my life, I had hardly any money to buy myself new clothes, never mind some guy from Montana! So I disregarded the letter and thought nothing more about it. However, about four weeks later, he wrote again telling me how disappointed he was that I hadn't sent him any cash. He explained that he was so heartbroken that he had tried to commit suicide, hoping that his death would make it into the local newspaper. He thought that I would feel guilty about it if someone told me about the story. I was shocked and found the whole thing disturbing. Why would someone want to die in order to give me a guilty conscience? Apparently, he tied his feet to a railway line and laid down on the track, waiting for the next train to end it all for him, but two rail workers spotted him and raced to his rescue. Despite pleas to leave him alone, they managed to untie him. In his letter he wrote that because he'd been given another chance he wanted to give me the opportunity to make amends and that he'd still gratefully accept any cash that I gave to him. I ignored the letter, but I do hope that the man hasn't tried to commit suicide again.

I would honestly love to help everyone in Bulgaria who is in need, but it is impossible to do so, even though people who know me will tell you that I am a generous person. I give a fair chunk of my salary to different charities, and Paulina spends much of her time studying newspapers and adverts looking for people we can help out. We're in a privileged situation and try to make a difference, even if it's a small one.

I received another letter just before Christmas 2001. It came from a couple in Bulgaria that wanted to move to Glasgow to open a church for Bulgarian people in Scotland. Their only problem was that they reckoned they'd need about £20,000 to get the church up and running, and they wanted me to provide them with the cash. Oh, and for the money I was to give them they would name the church after me as a thank you! Again, it was another request that I found difficult to see the merits of. Not every letter from my homeland is like that, though. A lot of Bulgarian people take the time to write complimentary things, and if they supply a name and address, I send them an autographed photo of me or the team.

The Celtic fans usually write good letters, and I often wonder if I'll ever be able to understand what the club means to them. I'd like to stay at Celtic for the rest of my career, but football is a business, and I may end up being sold to another club if they offer a good fee for me. I really hope that doesn't happen, and as long as Celtic are ambitious, I'll be happy to stay. The only thing that could make me want to leave is if we don't move from the SPL within the next few years. I'd like to get the chance to sample playing down south, but, first and foremost, I'd like it to be with Celtic.

I want to stay because the club is huge. We have supporters all over the world who have a strong emotional attachment to the club. The turnout for former captain Tom Boyd's testimonial match against Manchester United is a good example of the kind of support that we get from the Celtic fans. There were around 50,000 there for his game, which was truly incredible. I hope that if I stay with the club for that long I can experience what Tom went through that night.

It's special to play in front of our fans at every home game, and when I'm getting ready in the dressing-room before a match, I get excited about going out there and doing my best to entertain them. They definitely save their best for Old Firm games, and when you're on the pitch, it sounds like complete madness all around the stadium. The boys can hardly hear each other, and you have to go right up to a player and shout into his ear to make yourself heard. It's also an impossible task for the manager to get instructions to players on the pitch, which I suppose can only be a good thing if he's trying to give you a hard time!

Another fantastic thing about the unique atmosphere at Celtic Park is that opposition players can freeze. I think that happened to a couple of Valencia players when we played against them in the UEFA Cup game back in 2001. It was a huge game, and Henrik Larsson put us one up, but it was just unfortunate that we couldn't score a second to take us through.

You Can Call Me Stan

Our supporters are terrific, and I enjoy going out to meet them at functions and Player of the Year nights. That wasn't always the case, mind you. I remember my first supporters' do was during my first two months at the club. Jonathan Gould couldn't make it, and I was told to be at Paisley for six o'clock to represent the club at the Davie Hay CSC Player of the Year night. I had never been to an event like that as we don't have such things in Bulgaria. I had no idea what to expect.

For some strange reason, I don't know why, I got it into my head that the do was at six o'clock in the morning. The club had organised a taxi to pick me up and take me to Paisley, so I was up at 5.15 a.m. to make sure I was clean and tidy for the big event and ready for my lift. I spoke to Brian Wilson about what to expect, and he'd told me I would have to sign autographs and pose for photographs with the supporters. He also told me a few key things that I should say. My English was non-existent at the time, so I memorised two key phrases: 'Hail, Hail' and 'Celtic supporters are the greatest supporters in the world'. Now, that might sound like I just trotted out that line for the sake of it and that I didn't really mean it, but that was not the case. I did mean it, it was just that I didn't know how to say it at that time.

Anyway, it got to about 6.15 a.m., but my taxi still hadn't turned up. I was nervous and kept checking my watch every 30 seconds. I phoned Brian, and he told me that the event started at six in the evening, but I was adamant that Jonathan had told me that it was six in the morning. I felt a bit stupid, and the boys slaughtered me in the dressing-room for a few days afterwards!

When I finally made it to the function, I was walking into the unknown. Brian came with me, and we were greeted in a side room by a committee of about eight or nine people. I naively thought that no one else was going to turn up, and I didn't feel too nervous. My mood changed, though, when one of the members asked me to make a speech, but I had my two phrases all ready in my head.

I was just about to start when I noticed that it was really noisy outside the room. I could hear singing and the sound of loads of people enjoying a party. I asked what was going on and was told that the fans were starting to arrive for the function. All of a sudden, I went from preparing to speak in front of a few people in a small room to the prospect of having to speak to around 400 Paisley Celtic fans! I was terrified. Seconds later, I was told to get ready to make my entrance into the main hall. I was really scared and wanted to leave, but once I went out there, the fans gave me a standing ovation. They made me feel at ease, and I managed to get through it.

I have been to loads more functions since and now enjoy going out to meet the supporters. They go out of their way to cheer us on, so we have to make an effort to give them something back. The more fans that I meet, the more that it astounds me just how big this club is. It is steeped in tradition, and it's an honour for me to be part of it. For example, when I think back to the 'Lisbon Lions' winning the European Cup in 1967, it reminds me of what this club is all about and what it's achieved.

During my time in Scotland I have made it my business to find out as much about Celtic as possible. I have a genuine appetite for knowledge about Celtic and can reel off several success stories that the club has enjoyed down the years. Of course, the obvious ones are the 1967 European Cup win and the defeat to Feyenoord in the 1970 European Cup final. It's amazing to think that Celtic came so close to winning that famous trophy twice in four seasons. However, the club has had many more special moments during the last 25 years, on top of their European successes. I've enjoyed finding out about the 1979 League decider against Rangers when the Bhoys won 4–2 and the 1988 Double in the club's centenary season. That Double was clinched at Hampden in the Scottish Cup final against Dundee United when Frank McAvennie scored two goals in the final minutes to give Celtic a 2–1 win. I have also made friends with many Celtic supporters, and they have been a good source of information about the glory days, going back as far as the 1957 League Cup final when the team beat Rangers 7–1. The club has had such a long and glorious past that I find out new things about Celtic almost every day.

Those times will never be forgotten by Celtic people or by the guys who played their part on those memorable occasions such as Billy McNeill, Jimmy Johnstone, Danny McGrain, Tommy Gemmell, Kenny Dalglish and Paul McStay. The club recently introduced its own Hall of Fame, and it's a great idea to remember and honour some of the great names that have played a part in Celtic's rich history. Henrik Larsson was voted into the 'Greatest Celtic Team' alongside players like Jimmy Johnstone, Billy McNeill, Kenny Dalglish, Danny McGrain and Bertie Auld. I know Henrik was so proud to have made it into such illustrious company and have his name written into the club's history books.

I often see different members of the Lisbon Lions in and around Celtic Park on match days, and it reminds me of their incredible achievement in beating Inter Milan 2–1 on that glorious day in Lisbon. I use it to spur me on and dream that maybe one day I can emulate their tremendous feat. Of course, it won't be easy, but I will never stop trying to bring success to this club. Winning trophies at the highest level has to be the aim of every footballer, and I have to believe that I am capable of doing so.

The thought of winning the European Cup for the club and trying to make it into the Celtic Hall of Fame really motivates me, although I accept I'm a million miles away from both. But I never say never, and it would be very special to come back to Glasgow later on in life with my children and grandchildren to show them my place in the history of Celtic Football Club and the contribution that I made.